THE TIGERS OF '68

THE TIGERS OF '68

*Baseball's
Last Real
Champions*

George Cantor

TAYLOR TRADE PUBLISHING

*Lanham • Boulder • New York •
Toronto • Plymouth, UK*

Dedicated to everyone who, holding tightly to their father's hand, walked into a ballpark for the first time and fell hopelessly in love with a game and a team for the rest of their lives.

Published by Taylor Trade Publishing
An imprint of Rowman & Littlefield
4501 Forbes Boulevard, Suite 200, Lanham, Maryland 20706
www.rowman.com

10 Thornbury Road, Plymouth PL6 7PP, United Kingdom

Distributed by NATIONAL BOOK NETWORK

Photos provided by Richard Bak

British Library Cataloguing in Publication Information Available

The hardback edition of this book was previously cataloged by the Library of Congress as follows:

Cantor, George, 1941–
   The Tigers of '68 : baseball's last real champions / George Cantor
     p. cm.
   Includes index.
   1. Detroit Tigers (Baseball team)—History. I. Title.
   GV875.D6C35   1997
   796.357'64'0977434—dc21   96-29580

ISBN 978-1-58979-928-8 (pbk. : alk. paper)
ISBN 978-1-58979-929-5 (electronic)

♾™ The paper used in this publication meets the minimum requirements of American National Standard for Information Sciences—Permanence of Paper for Printed Library Materials, ANSI/NISO Z39.48-1992.

Printed in the United States of America

CONTENTS

The Tigers of '68

Preface

In his own way, Brent Musberger is as responsible for this book as anyone else. The veteran sportscaster was then baseball writer for Chicago's *American,* and he was lined up to be hired for the same job at the *Detroit Free Press* in early 1966. But he backed out, and the paper, to my utter astonishment, picked me.

The opening in Detroit developed when Joe Falls, the longtime beat writer, was given a column. Most newsmen understood that the *American* was not likely to survive, and Brent seemed delighted at the chance to get out. But two weeks before spring training, he changed his mind, deciding that broadcasting might offer him a better escape hatch from the coming shipwreck.

It was a great choice. But it left the *Free Press* with no one to go to Florida with the Tigers. No one but me, a desperation choice. I had all of three years professional experience as a journalist, none as a sportswriter. I had just been moved to days on the news desk and was starting to get good assignments. But knowing of my interest (well, let's be honest—my absorption in baseball), a few senior editors suggested my name for the job. When the chance came, I grabbed it. And without the slightest idea of what I was doing, I boarded a plane for Florida and became a baseball writer.

I was so out of it that I wore a suit and tie to the first workout. At the age of twenty-four, I was the youngest beat writer with a big league team. Most of the players were my contemporaries in age, though, and my paycheck was about as large as most of theirs. We traveled on the same planes and buses, stayed in the same hotels. There was an easy intimacy and an access between writers and athletes that vanished from all sports long ago.

I worked the baseball beat for four seasons, and it was the turning point of my career. While holding the best job in the world, I learned to be a newspaperman. I learned how to write under pressure, how to develop stories on a beat, how to get information from individuals who were not always happy to talk to me. Most journalists must learn these things in police stations or courthouses. My training ground was a ballpark.

And as a bonus I got to cover a world championship, watch the ballclub I had rooted for since childhood win the World Series. When Jim Northrup's triple cleared Curt Flood's head in the seventh inning of the seventh game, it took all the journalistic restraint I had in my body to keep from jumping up and screaming—as I knew my brother and father were doing in the family room back in Detroit. Instead, I simply said quietly, "Oh, my God," and began thinking of a lead for the biggest story I had ever written.

The 1968 Tigers never repeated. Over the years, their achievements have slipped into a memory hole between the exploits of the 1967 Red Sox of the Impossible Dream and the 1969 Miracle Mets. These were the darlings of the East Coast media and a Detroit team just couldn't compare. But in Michigan, and wherever Tigers fans are scattered, the memory lives on, as fresh as yesterday's box score. This was a team that wrapped itself around their souls and never left. Even today, when you talk with them about some of the events of that year, they are sometimes moved to tears.

Ten members of that team settled permanently in the Detroit area, and so in a very real sense they never left the scene of their triumph. But it's more than that. It is the way they won, the times in which they won, the personalities who did the winning. Like the hook from a Smokey Robinson hit, they bring back the emotions of a specific time and place with a clarity that gladdens the heart.

But they were really not part of those times, at all. When I returned to writing news in 1970, I felt that I had stepped out of a spacecraft, landed on another planet. One of the first assignments given to me was to interview a young man who had dodged the draft and was seeking sanctuary in a Detroit church. He told me that his needs had been taken care of by "The Movement." I had no idea what he was talking about. The world had undergone a change almost beyond my comprehension. Pot was passed around routinely at parties. Women were asserting their equality. The negroes who existed before I went into the baseball job had vanished, replaced by blacks, and a lot of them were pissed. But baseball had gone on as always. It may have been the 70s on the calendar, but back in the ballpark it felt eternally like 1938, with Gehrig waiting on deck.

This book is an attempt to put the summer of 1968 into a historical perspective. To talk to the middle-aged men who once were heroes and ask about their lives and what that season meant to them. For them, as well as for me, it was probably the best summer of their lives. For baseball, overwhelmed by change, most of it not for the better, it may well have been the last good season.

THE TIGERS OF '68

CHAPTER 1

Light My Fire

When Mickey Lolich walked to the mound for his pregame warm-ups, the cloud was barely a smudge, a dirty puff of smoke rising behind the left-field light towers. All through the afternoon it grew wider and higher as it climbed into the clear, summer sky. Only those spectators seated high in the upper deck along the first baseline could see it. Most of the 43,000 spectators who sat through the Tigers-Yankees doubleheader on this muggy July 23, 1967, had no idea what was going on.

Detroit was burning down.

About thirteen hours before Lolich threw his first pitch, Detroit police had raided a blind pig, an illegal after-hours gambling establishment, on 12th Street. Within minutes, a crowd gathered at the site, which was in a busy commercial area less than three miles north of the ballpark. When the cops tried to shoulder their way to the police wagons with their collars, they found themselves surrounded by angry black onlookers. It was a sultry night. The crowd refused to move. There was some jostling. Threats were shouted. Then someone threw a rock.

In that instant, 12th Street exploded. The police retreated before the onslaught. Phones rang in the homes of the city's police commissioner and mayor within minutes. Many of the small businesses in the area were already in flames, their front windows lying in shattered slivers on the pavement and their stock carried off. A few homes and apartment buildings on the adjacent residential blocks were burning, too. A call was put in to John Conyers, the area's congressman. He was one of the first black men sent to Washington by Detroit voters and the most popular African-American politician in the city. Conyers hurried to the scene, mounted a flatbed truck, and in reasoned tones appealed for calm. A rock came flying out of the furious crowd, and then another. Conyers leaped from the truck and sped out of the area.

The mob surged south on 12th Street, driving back a line of police who were trying to form a defensive wall with their shields. A newspaper reporter walking behind police was cut by a shard of flying glass and, with blood streaming from a head wound, was carried to nearby Henry Ford Hospital. William Serrin, who later would cover the labor beat for *The New York Times*, kept his bloodstained shirt as a souvenir of that morning for years afterward. Detroit's two dailies were already printing their fat Sunday editions when the riot began. When the papers landed on the doorsteps of more than a million homes that morning, they carried not a word of the disturbance. Radio and television stations, operating with skeleton staffs on a Sunday, were asked to downplay the situation. So when fans and players started driving to Tiger Stadium, almost none of them knew what was happening on 12th Street.

They did know that the Tigers were in a hell of a pennant race. Five teams were bunched within five games of each other on this July afternoon. Four of them—Detroit, Boston, Chicago, and Minnesota—each had taken turns at the top, and California was driving hard, right behind them. One team would put together a streak, claw a path into first place, and then fall back, sometimes all the way to fourth. The Tigers were now running third. They had fought injuries all season long. Al Kaline was down with a broken finger. Willie Horton had missed a month and a half with a bad Achilles tendon. Jim Northrup was afflicted with the mumps. In addition, Denny McLain was pitching poorly, almost as if distracted by other matters, and Lolich hadn't won in two months. Still, the Tigers hung on, and the city, without a pennant for twenty-two years, was swept up in the drama of the race. The feeling was that if the Tigers could get healthy before time ran out, they were, far and away, the most talented team in the American League.

Detroit was known as one of baseball's best cities. The Tigers were adored in good years and bad. So all through the early summer big crowds jammed the ballpark, sensing that this could be the season when, at last, their wait would be rewarded.

Lolich, although in the middle of a terrible slump, kept the Tigers in the first game of the doubleheader with New York. But two late errors gave the Yankees a 4–2 win. It was the twenty-six-year-old left-hander's tenth consecutive loss, a team record. Thoroughly disgusted, he dressed between games and prepared for his long, lonely motorcycle ride home, to the semirural town of Washington in Detroit's far northeastern suburbs. Almost as soon as he arrived he would be notified to report for duty to his National Guard unit. The pitcher was being mobilized for riot duty in the city.

Detroit rallied to win the second game, 7–3, behind the relief pitching of John Hiller and Mike Marshall. That's the way it had gone all season. Win one, lose one. Never good enough to take control of the race, or bad enough to fall out of it. Horton's third-inning homer put the Tigers ahead for keeps. By that time, the dark cloud in the distance was growing steadily. It now extended all the way behind the center-field stands. The press box knew what was going on a few dozen blocks away, and sportswriters looked apprehensively at the swirling smoke. A New York columnist surveyed the scene. "Maybe they're just getting the merchandise together for Willie Horton Day," he said. No one laughed. Detroit was burning down. It would never be the same city again.

But the games went on that day. It was as if the stadium was wrapped in a cocoon, untouched by the catastrophe that was engulfing the city. This was not the first urban riot of the late '60s, and it certainly would not be the last. However, with forty-three deaths before order was restored, it was the deadliest. In this year there were antiwar demonstrations throughout the country. The youth of America were in the midst of their long, strange, transforming trip. Drugs permeated every campus. Young people with flowers in their hair and a blankness behind their eyes aimlessly strummed guitars and spent the summer groovin' in city parks. The culture was in upheaval. The Beatles and Timothy Leary and the Black Panthers. It seemed that revolution was coming in on the next strong gust of wind. In a hundred ways, large and small, the country appeared to be coming apart. "Come on, baby, light my fire," sang Jim Morrison over every radio.

Baseball went on, unknowing and untouched. Mickey Mantle still hit third for the Yanks. Willie Mays roamed center for the Giants. Most ballparks did not even permit rock music to be played between innings. At Tiger Stadium, the organist was told that the liveliest music permitted was a polka. A few ballplayers would retreat to a corner of the trainer's room and pop "greenies," diet pills that induced a quick energy surge. But beyond that, with the notable exceptions of alcohol and nicotine, drugs were unknown. The Vietnam protests and rallies, love-ins, and acid trips were part of a parallel reality, one that did not intrude on baseball's space. A player watching TV footage of a campus antiwar rally—attended by students with long hair and flowing robes and Native American regalia—would turn away from the screen, shake his head, and mutter: "Fuckin' Halloween." There was no place for this in baseball.

By the time the last fly ball of the doubleheader settled into the glove of left fielder Lennie Green, it was after 7:00 P.M. Detroit did not observe daylight savings time, so light already was starting to fail. Twilight was made even deeper by billowing columns of smoke that ascended in an unbroken wall north of the ballpark. The public address announcer gave the final totals for the second game. "For Detroit, seven runs, twelve hits, no errors; for New York, three runs, nine hits, and one error. Winning pitcher, Hiller. Losing pitcher, Peterson. The Detroit Baseball Club has been advised that the Grand River, Linwood, and Fenkell bus lines will not be operating this evening. Please drive safely."

Not operating! The streets the buses traveled were going up in flame. Smoke was pouring in dense waves across the Lodge Freeway. Homeward-bound drivers had to slow to an anxious crawl to get through. Gunfire was heard throughout the city, and the 10th Precinct was, for all purposes, under siege by snipers. A woman standing at a second floor window at a motel near the General Motors Building was shot dead by an unknown gunman. Squads of looters were racing out every major artery of the city, randomly breaking into stores and setting some of them afire. As darkness fell, flames illuminated a dozen neighborhoods. The situation was far beyond the control of police and National Guard units. But Michigan's Governor George Romney hesitated for hours before requesting federal troops because the phone call had to go to his political enemy, President Lyndon B. Johnson. Mayor Jerome Cavanagh, one of the young stars of the Democratic Party, was watching his reputation and ambitions turn to ashes in Detroit's streets. All this was breaking loose in the world outside baseball's cocoon. But all that the Tigers saw fit to tell their spectators was that some bus lines weren't running, as if nothing more was going on than a drivers' strike or an especially troublesome water main break.

Motown was burning down.

By nightfall, Lolich had returned to the city in full combat gear, assigned to guard a public works supply depot on the West Side. He belonged to the 191st Michigan National Guard unit, which ran a motor pool. What exactly his motor pool was supposed to do in this supply depot, miles from the scene of any rioting, was never made clear to him. He did know, however, that he was hungry. All he'd had to eat all day had been a snack between games, and because he'd lost again he hadn't had much of an appetite.

"All I knew was that I was starved and so were the other guys," he said. "We'd all been told to report immediately, and most of us hadn't been able to grab dinner. So after a while, when it looked like nothing was happening where we were, I decided to try and find someplace open and get some food. The streets were empty, and I was just walking along, with my rifle out in front of me, the way we were taught to patrol. Finally, I found this little hamburger place that had stayed open. The guy was really glad to see me, and he loaded me up with burgers, fries, and shakes. The only problem was I had no way to carry them back. If I slung my rifle over my back I'd be violating military policy. I could be court-martialed or something. So the storeowner sent his kid back with me. He carried the food, and I was his armed escort. If anyone had tried to grab those burgers, man, they'd have been in for the fight of their life. That's how I spent my first night on duty in the riot.

"Later on, they transferred me to police headquarters in downtown Detroit. Now that was a little scary, watching those wagons come in and unload the prisoners, one right after the other. Some of them were in really bad shape. The major in my unit decided that me and him should go out and patrol the surrounding streets. Nothing was moving downtown. It was a ghost town. Since I was the top-rated marksman in the unit, I suggested he drive while I rode shotgun. And wouldn't you know he stopped at the red lights! There's no other car on the street for miles, snipers are all over the place, and this guy is stopping on the red. 'Ahhh, sir,' I told him. 'Don't you think it would be better if we just kept moving?' 'Oh, sure. Right, Mickey,' he said and floored it. But that was about as nervous as it got for me."

By this time, the Baltimore Orioles, who were scheduled to

start a three-game series in Detroit on Monday, had been told to stay home. Instead, the Tigers and city officials had come up with a wonderful plan. They would save the city with baseball. The games would be switched to Baltimore and put on television. Everyone would be so caught up in the pennant race that they would stop looting and watch the games on TV. It was brilliant in its simplicity. After all, what American didn't prefer baseball to rioting any day?

The sad part was that this plan was regarded as realistic. There was absolutely no understanding of what caused the riots or of the depth of passions that they had unleashed. Baseball was still convinced that it had the power to douse the flames and rescue Detroit.

The Tigers flew to Baltimore on Tuesday and took the field for a night game as Detroit reeled through its third straight day of gunfire and death. TV cameras beamed the pictures from Memorial Stadium back to Michigan. The teams battled to a 0–0 tie into the second inning. The Tigers put two men on base with Joe Sparma coming to bat. Then it started to rain.

The grounds crew reacted as if rain on a July night in Baltimore was an absolute meteorological stunner. While the playing field turned into a dismal pool of goo, crew members hesitated, stumbled, slipped, ran into each other, and appeared to be auditioning for *The Keystone Cops Go to the Ballgame*.

The Detroit television crew, mindful of the critical role it was playing in this great social drama, desperately looked for someone to put on the air before viewers got it into their heads to start rioting again. The crew settled on Eddie Stanky, the manager of the White Sox. It was not a fortuitous choice. Stanky's team was spending an off day in Washington, so he had driven over to watch his rivals from Detroit. He was a small, excitable man, easily roused to a towering fury by imagined slights. The previous weekend, the *Detroit Free Press* had carried an extended question-and-answer interview with him. Usually, bad grammar and malapropisms are cleaned up in such an interview. But Stanky had been so abrasive that the two interviewers, Joe Falls and I, decided to let it run just as he said it. So the text contained gems like: "He couldn't hit the sidewalk with a bag of beets." and "The word 'defeat' is not in my category."

Stanky was furious. As he started his TV interview, he spotted me observing the proceedings. That did it. He instantly went off on a tirade, blasting me and Falls and even the baseball writer for the *Detroit News*, who had nothing whatsoever to do with the story. He said we were malicious rascals, lying troublemakers. He said we were bad for baseball. Stanky went on and on, growing more agitated by the minute. The TV producer instinctively understood that this was not the right sort of thing to broadcast to an already overheated populace. He got Stanky off the air as fast as he could and focused the cameras instead on the rain pouring down on the tarp, which hadn't quite made it all the way to the first baseline. The field was now an unplayable swamp, and the game was called off after an hour. The great rescue mission had failed, a victim of recalcitrant weather. The rioting in Detroit went on, eventually winding down of its own accord. And the 1967 season spun itself out to its own sad conclusion in a cruelly wounded city.

CHAPTER 2

A Pennant Squandered

It should never have come to this. The Tigers knew it. On the last, cold October evening of the 1967 season, with the home crowd pleading for one more rally, just one more big hit, they stood three outs from oblivion. If they lost, the race was over. Boston would conclude an incredible comeback season by winning its first pennant in twenty-one years. If they won, Boston would have to fly to Detroit for a playoff game, winner take all, the next day. The Red Sox sat in their Fenway Park clubhouse, seven hundred miles away, listening to Detroit radio announcer Ernie Harwell's voice piping in the transmission over a Boston station.

The California Angels held an 8–5 lead in the ninth. But it never should have come to this. Two weeks before, the Tigers had been tied for first place with Boston and Minnesota, and Chicago was just 1½ games behind. It was going to be the tightest finish in American League history. This is what the Tigers had waited for. They had claimed all along that their talent would be the decisive factor down the stretch. But four times in the next eleven games they blew leads in the eighth inning or later. Their bull pen failed. They made mistakes, horrible mental blunders. McLain turned up with a mysterious foot injury and fell out of the starting rotation. Manager Mayo Smith benched slumping first baseman Norm Cash, who was booed unmercifully by unforgiving Tiger Stadium crowds. He was replaced by fading National League star Eddie Mathews, picked up from Houston in an August waiver deal.

Then, just as in Baltimore during the riots, even the weather failed the Tigers. The closing four-game series against California had been scheduled over four days. But on Thursday and Friday, drenching early autumn rains fell on Detroit without a break. The games were rained out and had to be made up as two consecutive doubleheaders on the weekend. The Tigers would have to win three of the four games to tie for the league lead.

The delay enabled the rejuvenated Lolich to pitch the first game Saturday. He threw a shutout, his second straight white-wash and ninth win in ten decisions since the day of the riots ten weeks before. But the bull pen blew a four-run lead in the second game. Now there was no more margin. One more loss and it was over.

There were 15,000 empty seats at the ballpark for the deciding games Sunday. Attendance had fallen off sharply after the riots. The team would draw only 1.4 million people for the season. In 1961, when the Tigers stayed in the race until early September, 1.6 million had come to the ballpark. The attendance difference between those two years was the fear factor.

Detroit was a wounded, suspicious city. Many streets were still in ruins, the burned-out husks of stores and houses dotting block after block. Suburbanites stopped coming into the city. The fastest growing plant in Detroit that summer was a "For Sale" sign on the front lawn. What had been a slow, steady out migration to the suburbs turned into a stampede after July 23. With images of the riots burned into their memories, thousands of Detroiters decided they'd had enough. They took whatever price they could get for their homes and fled. Accusations flew across a widening racial divide. An understanding that civic leaders thought had been well crafted between the races turned out to be made of hot air, with neither value nor meaning.

Still, the city hung on the fate of the Tigers. Sparma stopped California in Sunday's opener. Then McLain, who hadn't pitched in thirteen days, walked to the mound for game two. He had fallen asleep on his living room couch one night while watching TV, he said, when he was awakened by the rattle of a trash can. He thought it was a raccoon. When he tried to leap from the couch to investigate, he said, his foot was asleep and wouldn't support his weight. He fell and twisted his ankle, he said. It was a good story, typically McLain in its bizarre sequence of events. Not until two years later would a darker version emerge.

McLain had not won a game since August 29 and was 17–16 for the year. The Tigers had expected much more after his twenty-win season in 1966. His appearance was brief this time out. The Angels drove him out in the third while taking a 4–3 lead. They continued the assault on every pitcher Detroit put in, running the margin to 8–3. Dick McAuliffe chopped two runs off the lead with a hit in the seventh. But now it was the ninth, with just three outs to go and extinction staring right at them.

It had turned ugly. While pursuing a pop foul, Mathews near-ly stumbled over a news photographer. Photographers were allowed to work on the field then, and when the photographer lost sight of the ball he did what he was supposed to do—stay in a crouch and allow the players to get around him. But Mathews, not used to the ground rules in Detroit, nearly dropped the ball as he dodged to avoid the photographer. Then Mathews stopped and hurled the ball right at the feet of the photographer, as the crowd booed.

By the ninth, there was no more booing. The crowd was beg-ging its team to fight back into it. When Freehan led off with a double and Don Wert drew a walk to put the tying run at bat, hope lurched convulsively back into the ballpark. The Angels brought in George Brunet, a left-handed journeyman who beat the Tigers with disturbing regularity as a starter. He got pinch hitter Jim Price on an infield fly. That brought up McAuliffe. As he left the on-deck circle, a fan leaped to the roof of the Detroit dugout and bowed in an attitude of prayer. He appeared to be a drunk, out of control. But those sitting closest to him could see that he was sobbing.

McAuliffe, the most relentless competitor on the team, had enjoyed a good season after being switched from shortstop to second base. Second was a far more comfortable position for him on defense, and the improvement was apparent on offense, as well. He had, in fact, hit into just one double play all year long. He now did it for a second time—a hard grounder directly at the second baseman. And just like that, the long season was over.

In Boston, the Red Sox leaped from their seats in the clubhouse, hugging each other, spewing champagne around the room, dancing in wild celebration. Manager Dick Williams, who had brought his young son with him to wait out the score in Detroit, embraced the boy. "Don't ever forget this," he murmured to him. "Don't ever forget this."

In Detroit, the lights were going out all over the stadium. In the tunnel from the dugout, Green turned and fired a baseball at a TV crew filming the Tigers' retreat from the field. Mayo Smith ran into his old friend, California manager Bill Rigney, in the cold stadium corridor outside the clubhouse. The two men hugged. "I'm sorry, Mayo," said Rigney. "Naah," said the Detroit manager. "I'm proud of you. You fought us all the way." When the Tigers clubhouse doors finally opened, most players were still seated at their lockers, heads slumped in numbed resignation. Many of them had been crying. "All summer long it was, 'Oh, well, we'll get 'em tomorrow,'" said Freehan, his big frame sagging in weary defeat. "Now there's no more tomorrow. I can't believe it." They were convinced that the best team had not won. They would now have four and half months to think about that.

CHAPTER 3

Springtime in Lakeland

The players started drifting into Lakeland in mid-February. The central Florida town had been the Tigers' spring base since 1934 (aside from a three-year break because of World War II travel restrictions), the longest continuous association between any big league team and its Florida training site. Detroit had won its first pennant in twenty-five years immediately upon moving there and thus saw no good reason ever to move again.

After the war, the Tigers purchased a tract of land that had been used as a base to train British naval pilots. The team converted the land into Tigertown, a complex of diamonds and dormitories where every player in the entire minor league system was trained and domiciled. It was the first such operation in baseball. The Tigers felt it created an organizational unity. Detroit believed in its farm system with an almost religious fervor. It was convinced that a core of players, all indoctrinated in the same basic approach and techniques, was essential in building a winner. Of the twenty-five men who eventually formed the roster of the 1968 Tigers, fifteen had come through the Tigertown complex. About half of them arrived in the majors within a year or two of each other in the mid-60s. They were called "the Boys from Syracuse," which was then the system's top AAA affiliate.

"It was like family," Jim Northrup says of that group. "We barbecued together with our wives and kids. We partied together. When we had problems we talked to each other. Hell, we even loaned each other money when things got tight—although we'd try and run the other way when McLain came along. He was constantly looking for a few bucks 'to get something for Sharyn.' It wasn't a loan with Denny. It was more like a gift. But by the time we reached the bigs we had known each other for years. It was a closeness I don't believe can exist anywhere in professional sports anymore."

Lakeland in 1968 was not the Florida of the travel posters. After Walt Disney World opened in the '70s a few miles east on Interstate 4, Lakeland joined the rest of Florida. Condominiums, malls, traffic, and high growth have transformed the place. But in the spring of 1968 it was still part of the Deep South in its drowsy ambience, racial attitudes, and sense of itself. There were two movie theaters in town, not counting the drive-in, which primarily showed films that bore titles like *Preacher Man Meets Widder Woman*. The nearest ABC television affiliate came in as a ghostly flicker on most sets. Finding an out-of-town newspaper or a corned beef sandwich could involve a trek that lasted for miles. Lakeland was in another dimension from the glitzy Gold Coast resorts or even from the beachfront towns on the gulf. This was citrus country, the top orange-producing county in America, with a little phosphate mining thrown in. Still, there was a certain charm about the town and the string of small lakes around which it had grown. Spring training was a soothing, unvarying cycle of golf at the country club, dinners at the yacht club, black bean soup at the Cuban restaurants in nearby Tampa, and the annual chamber of commerce steak-

and-shrimp cookout in a hangar at the old air base. For the Tigers and their general manager, Jim Campbell, who prided himself on running a conservative organization both fiscally and socially, it was bliss.

The Holiday Inn, where team officials, rookies, and media stayed, had been open for just three years and was regarded as the height of luxury—which it was when compared with the former team hotel, with its front porch full of rocking chairs that appeared to have been broken in by Stonewall Jackson's troops. This was also the third season of operation for Joker Marchant Stadium, home field for Tigers spring games. Its odd name was a tribute to Lakeland's director of parks and recreation, a man who favored cowboy boots and Stetson hats and looked as if he knew some really great stories, if he ever chose to tell them. He never quite got around to that, though. It seemed that the funniest thing he ever saw was when a young journalist, trying to file a story at the Western Union office, absent mindedly walked into the appliance store next door. "Son, were you going to send that story over a washing machine?" Joker would ask whenever he saw the young man for years afterward, almost howling in glee. "Were you fixin' to give it to a refrigerator?"

Although the Civil Rights Act of 1964 had legally ended segregation, Lakeland remained a town fixed in its racial attitudes. There was a black part of town, and there was a white one. There was no overlap. The team's black players found it difficult to find acceptable accommodations for their families, so they lived at the Holiday Inn. The Tigers ran a bus service for them to the black neighborhood in the evening. Most white veterans lived with their families in a motel on the Old Tampa Road. It was far from luxurious, but it was the best of its kind in Lakeland.

The organization had not been idle after the crushing failure of 1967. Mostly, it had been occupied attempting to trade McLain. There was a strong suspicion that the twenty-game season of 1966 was an aberration and that the 17–16 season of the next year was a closer measure of his real ability. More than that, there was the unmistakable perception that he was just not Tiger material. He was way too cocky, far too independent and outspoken. Moreover, he had failed the team down the stretch. He hadn't backed up the brag. But no trade was made. Warning flags about McLain were up all over the game, and no franchise was willing to make a commitment to him. Campbell had to settle for picking up Dennis Ribant, a pitcher who had impressed very few at Pittsburgh the previous year.

The entire pitching staff had been overhauled. Only five men remained from those who had left Florida with the team the previous spring. Campbell and Mayo Smith were convinced that the bull pen blew the pennant, and they were looking hard for strong, young arms. Otherwise, the team was unchanged from the one that had ended the 1967 season. McAuliffe was set at second, Wert at third, and Freehan behind the plate. There would be a four-man outfield rotation with Kaline, Horton, Northrup, and Stanley. Mayo wasn't quite sure how he would work that out. But both Kaline and Horton seemed to be injury prone, and he was sure that the rotation would take care of itself. At first base, there were Cash and Mathews. Cash was thirty-three and Mathews thirty-six, but both men lived hard off the field and appeared much older. The joke was that Mayo would throw the glove out at first base and see which one would pick it up—unless, of course, they couldn't straighten up again. Shortstop was troublesome. Ray Oyler was the designated starter and an excellent defensive player. But he was helpless as a hitter. Dick Tracewski was not quite as good on defense and hit somewhat better. Tom Matchick had shown some potential as a minor league hitter, but there were severe questions about his defense. That was where the Tigers needed help, and to fill that position they had shopped McLain. But they would have to make do with what they had.

Earl Wilson had won twenty-two games as a starter and appeared firm as the staff leader. Behind him would be Lolich, who had finished the 1967 season with an encouraging rush, and Sparma, coming off his best year at 16–9. And, of course, McLain.

McLain had arrived in Lakeland with orange hair ("I've been out in the sun a lot," he explained) and contact lenses to replace his thick spectacles. The cap was worn at a rakish angle, bill shading his eyes. He seemed unconcerned with the events of the previous season and reports of his impending departure. To all appearances, he was the same old Denny, sizing up the world with a knowing eye and finding it choice and fat.

But McLain, like every other veteran of 1967, had changed. Beneath the clubhouse laughter there was a new seriousness of intent. This was a team who had been through the grinder. The pain would never go away. But it had made them harder, tougher.

There were still the timeless, numbing spring routines to endure. But Mayo did not run a tight camp. Conditioning drills were minimal. Strength coaches were unknown then. Mike Marshall was a great believer in building up durability by lifting weights. But the twenty-five-year-old pitcher, who was working toward a Ph.D. at Michigan State University, was regarded as a moon man. The other players called him "Professor" and exchanged amused glances when he started talking about his theories of pitching, about using alternate sets of muscles on alternate days. In six more seasons, putting his theories into practice, he would break every record for appearances and innings pitched by a reliever. But that would be with the Dodgers. The Tigers could hardly wait to get rid of this crackpot.

Pitching coach Johnny Sain was not a believer in running. He believed that games were won with attitude and mental toughness. Although strong legs and healthy bodies were nice, they would not be the critical component when the game was on the line. So aside from a few serious athletes—Freehan, Stanley—it was not a camp that went in for serious athleticism.

The biggest event of the spring, as always, was introducing rookies to The Mongoose. This mysterious creature was kept in a large box, guarded by the assistant clubhouse attendant, a local lad named Gator. Newcomers to the team were told of this wonder in hushed tones and asked if they wanted to see it. Gator was then dispatched to get The Mongoose. He made a big show of struggling with the container and the creature thrashing around inside. A new player was told to look through a small peephole to see The Mongoose. When he did, Gator would release a spring, and a racoon tail would suddenly come flying out of a hole at the top of the box. The unsuspecting viewer's scream and wild leap, some of them attaining impressive measures in height and length, were always a highlight of the Lakeland experience and an initiation rite of the Tigers.

But something else was stirring, something much more powerful than The Mongoose. The Tigers had been installed as preseason favorites to win the pennant. No one in Lakeland disagreed. But they now knew something else, too. They knew what it would take to be the team left standing in October.

CHAPTER 4

Selling
the Dream

Running late. Gotta catch up. No time.

They had shut down a freeway on him in Detroit, and Bill Freehan was an hour late for his appointment. He was inspecting a factory he had invested in, trying to get back into the swing of the business world after six years off chasing a dream.

His company, Freehan-Bocci, was renting second-floor space above a beauty salon in Birmingham, a wealthy suburb of Detroit. Only temporary, he said. Only until he got himself organized again. Baseball memorabilia is the primary decor, but little about the setting is permanent.

At fifty-five, beneath the conservative businessman's suit and striped tie, he still has the athlete's walk. The drive that turned him into the best catcher in the American League for almost a decade still ticks away inside him, guided in other paths. He is seated behind a bare desk in a cubicle of an office defined by low, movable walls. He keeps his voice down to retain some privacy.

"The analogies between baseball and the business world are so apparent that they almost go without saying," he says. "When a team goes bad it's because people are trying to find fault, blaming somebody else, undermining the total effort. You have to learn what it's like to win, and that's true whether you're running a corporation or a ball club. And when you learn, you have to do everything you can to reinforce the lessons."

If Freehan sounds a little like the primary speaker at a motivational sales meeting, that was always part of the package. The first person he learned to motivate was himself. He had been thrust into a leadership role on a major league team before reaching his twenty-fifth birthday. He was given the job of calling pitches for some of the most talented and quirkiest individuals in the game. It had been more of a sales job than most observers ever guessed, a constant process of building up his own confidence, talking himself into success. But if you had to predict which of the '68 Tigers would do well after his career was over, top choice on most ballots would have been Freehan.

And yet, right in the middle of a successful career as a manufacturer's rep, with his finances assured and future clear, he tossed it aside for the chance to become baseball coach at the University of Michigan. Then six years later, just as abruptly, he quit.

"I'd never worked in an institutional setting before," he shrugs. "It was an adjustment I never got used to. But maybe it was something I had to get out of my system. I always wondered if I'd missed something, walking away from baseball when I did. I retired in 1976 and left the game completely—went right into business. So maybe the Michigan job was a chance to see how much I really missed it.

"I did in some ways. But you forget a lot of the negatives. That feeling of walking out of a ballpark after midnight, when everyone else has gone home and the only people left are the ones cleaning out the concession stands. I used to hate that feeling. There's nothing as lonely as an empty ballpark at night.

"After I made my decision at Michigan, it crossed my mind that maybe I should call the Tigers and see what was available. I knew they were going through some major reorganization and that there might be a place for me. I never made the call. It dawned on me that I was afraid they'd say yes. That image of walking out of the empty stadium—is that what I still wanted to be doing when I was fifty-five years old? I guess it was just time to make the final decision about what it is I want to do when I grow up."

That was the same phrase he had used to describe his situation during an interview conducted more than twenty years before, as he was preparing to retire from the Tigers. Growing up. Moving on. Easier to say than to complete.

Freehan started growing up only about three miles from this office, in the suburb of Royal Oak. He remembers clutching the money he earned on his paper route and taking the long bus ride to see games at Tiger Stadium. He was a Little League standout. In one All-Star game when a runner came in a little too hard at the plate, the two of them wound up rolling around in the dirt, flailing away at each other. The runner was Willie Horton.

Freehan's family moved to Florida just before Bill Freehan entered high school. He enrolled in a Catholic school in St. Petersburg and was a star in both baseball and football, with his choice of college scholarships. He wanted Notre Dame, but they told him he had to pick one sport or the other. So he settled on Western Michigan, then changed his mind at the last minute and went, instead, to Michigan.

"I went to a small high school in Florida," he explains, "and we were always getting beaten by the numbers. I wanted to be on the other side for a change."

At Michigan, Freehan was a starter at end as a sophomore football player. But it was in baseball that he excelled, hitting over .500 as a catcher during the 1961 Big 10 season. He signed a bonus contract with the Tigers and within two years was the regular catcher in Detroit.

Just before the end of spring training in 1968 he sat beside the pool of the Holiday Inn. It was a balmy April night, a soft breeze barely rustling the palms in the motel courtyard. The veterans always moved there for the last week of training, sending their families back to Detroit. It was a symbolic drawing-together before the start of the season, a gathering of strength by the team for the season ahead. Freehan understood, however, that this year was different. Of all the Tigers, he was the most bitter about the previous year's defeat. He had puzzled over it all winter, trying to understand what had happened.

"We got into the habit of thinking it was going to be automatic," he said. "Shoot, we knew we were the best. We thought we'd win easily. Maybe you have to learn that nothing comes to you. You have to take it.

"If it was just one game . . . hey, no problem. Anybody can get up for that. I did it as a football player all the time. But this is different. This is day after day after day. You can't get too high or you'll run yourself into the ground. But you've got to stay focused. Maybe it's because I'm a Detroit kid and I know what a pennant would have meant to this city. Maybe that's why it hurt as much as it did."

He was already balding in 1968, which made him look older. But there was an elfish twinkle, too, almost incongruous on a man of his size, like a leprechaun on steroids. He was the agitator, the back-of-the-bus wise guy, calling out, "Hey, Bussie, you've got it surrounded," when the driver keeps circling the wrong block in search of the team hotel. To a teammate wearing a white suit, he'd chortle, "Hey, two Fudgicles over here." But Freehan, more than any other single player, took 1968 on his shoulders as a personal mission.

"I always believed in competition rather than confrontation," he says in his tiny office. "I still do. I believe you build relationships to get the most out of people. That's the way I was as a catcher. I look at these computers and pitching charts they have in the dugouts now, and I have to laugh. The computer says pitch a guy this way so that's what you're supposed to do. But it's not that way. Can't be. You've got to understand everyone in the equation as an individual. Hitters adjust all the time, and you have to know what's going on inside your pitcher's head.

"You're always asking yourself questions about the pitcher.

'What do I do now? Is this the time to be blunt with this guy or to kid him along? What kind of stuff does he have? Is he losing it? Does it correspond to the book on this hitter?' What computer is going to tell you all that? That's absurd.

"It's all in the relationships. When Earl Wilson came over from Boston he was used to having Dick Radatz in the bull pen. He got into the habit of looking for help in the late innings. We didn't have any Radatz in Detroit. I had to get him to want to finish his games. With Lolich, it was a matter of confidence. He had one bad game and he was ready to change his whole style of pitching. His attitude changed entirely after the World Series. But before that he didn't have enough confidence in himself to get through trouble in the late innings. Afterwards, no problem. And Denny was Denny. We all believed in each other that season. Maybe Denny believed in himself a little bit more than anybody else.

"Now all the pitchers want raises if they have so many quality starts. Quality starts. When we played that meant you couldn't finish. It wasn't a stat you especially wanted to keep track of. Management would hammer you with it at negotiating time.

"I will say this about Mayo that season," Freehan says. "He gave me the authority to call the game I wanted. He wasn't big on signals from the dugout. We both had our ideas about things, and we'd go over them. But he'd listen to what I had to say. He wasn't trying to impose a viewpoint. Not every manager I played for was that way. Charlie Dressen always had to be in control, but I was just breaking in when I played for him. Billy Martin ran hot and cold. It dawned on me that it was all theatrics with Billy, all for effect.

"I remember once he brought in Hiller to pitch to Mike Epstein when he was with the As. Billy said he wanted nothing but curveballs. John threw a lousy curveball, and Epstein hit it into the seats to beat us. I'm at the locker after the game and reporters come up to me and starting asking me why I changed the sign. I looked up and said, 'Excuse me?' Billy had told them that I called for the curve and changed the pitching plan. I went into his office and shut the door and asked him what the hell was going on. 'They misunderstood what I was saying,' he said. Yeah, sure. But that's the kind of manager he was.

"Back then we were all bulletproof and going to live forever. We acted as if nothing could ever hurt us. Now the technology is so much better. The kids are prepared better than we were. They're bigger and stronger. But the motivation has changed. You didn't play to become a millionaire then. You think that's why Al Kaline and Eddie Mathews played the game? But I was an eyewitness to the start of the change. I was the player rep, one of the guys who was in on the decision to bring in Marvin Miller to be the attorney for the players' association. The key to the whole thing was that our attorney was twice as good as theirs.

"Now it's all different. Maybe it's because I'm on the other side, in business, but I think it's swung too far. I wonder sometimes why anyone would want to buy a big league franchise. Mike Ilitch spent $90 million to buy the Tigers and his annual return is something like one percent. That makes no sense at all. No one lays out that kind of money for that return."

Freehan still lives in the same home he bought as a player, in an area with some of the highest real estate values in Detroit. When his former teammate, the late Hank Aguirre, got the idea to start his company, Mexican Industries, to go after minority manufacturing contracts, Freehan was an investor. It was one of the firm's six factories that Freehan had just been looking over. The company is thriving. Life is good.

"What do I want to do when I grow up and get big?" he asks. It makes you wonder if the leprechaun lurking in his eyes will ever be entirely subdued by the white-shirted businessman with the accountant's mind. In an empty ballpark at night, you can still hear the roar of the past.

CHAPTER 5

A Matter of Race

Spring training ground to its tedious conclusion. By the first week in April, everyone was thoroughly sick of Lakeland, eager for real competition. All the good stories had been told several times. The brew had gone flat. Routines settled into stagnation. The only thing to look forward to was the bus ride to the Tampa airport and the flight home to Detroit.

The Tigers managed to win about as often as they lost that spring, finishing one game under .500. That's what a manager looks for from a contender in the exhibitions. Too many wins is the mark of mediocrity, matching regulars against the other teams' farmhands and building up an air of false confidence. Too many losses, on the other hand, is the mark of indifference. The last two games of this spring, however, quickened more than the usual interest. The Tigers would play a home-and-home series against the world champions, the St. Louis Cardinals. In these last days of spring training, regulars would fill both lineups. Each side intended to start top pitchers—Bob Gibson and Nelly Briles against Wilson and McLain. It wasn't quite the real thing but close enough to taste.

On the evening before the first of these games, Dr. Martin Luther King Jr. was murdered in Memphis.

The Tigers were among the last major league teams to inte-grate. Along with the Red Sox and Yankees, Detroit was known as a franchise that didn't especially welcome the coming of black ballplayers. The first one hadn't reached Tiger Stadium until 1958, more than a decade after Jackie Robinson first stepped on the field wearing a Dodgers uniform. Even then, the move won no cheers from the city's large black community. The player who integrated the Tigers was Ozzie Virgil, who came from the Dominican Republic. It was, black fans pointed out, not quite the same thing.

Within three years, however, the Tigers had traded for Milwaukee's star center fielder, Billy Bruton, and had brought up rookie second baseman Jake Wood. They hit one-two in Detroit's 1961 lineup and added some speed to a team that was notorious-ly slow. Bruton and Wood set the table for the sluggers hitting behind them. The fans were delighted, urging them raucously to run each time they got on base. They combined for fifty-two steals, almost as many as the entire team had managed the pre-vious year.

By 1968, there were three African-Americans on the team. Horton had come off the streets of Detroit, a local legend even as a high school star because of his long home runs. Gates Brown had been scouted behind the walls of the Ohio State Penitentiary. His story of personal redemption also made him a popular figure in Detroit. The third man was Earl Wilson. He was obtained from Boston midway through the 1966 season and turned into the team's most effective pitcher, going 35–17 since the trade.

To all appearances, there was no racial divide on the Tigers. Gates was a regular in endless games of tonk (which vaguely resembled gin rummy) and pinochle. The games were played on airplanes and in hotel rooms, with a core of Brown, McLain, John Hiller, Pat Dobson, and an ever-changing cast of others. McLain was especially welcomed. He played cards so poorly that Jake Wood nicknamed him "Dolphin," because he was regarded as a fish on the hook. Racial bantering in the card games and in the clubhouse was low key and went both ways. Gates was often quoted as saying that his friend, Horton, had had a schedule in high school that had included "taking math, history, and overcoats." A few seasons before, Horton had been accidentally cut on the hand while Gates was cleaning his spikes with a knife. There was a racist edge to the whispers about that because both men were competing for the starting job in left field. In reality, the two were close friends, and Gates was mortified by the accident.

Wilson was a bit more aloof. He was a tall, almost regal man. Gates referred to him as the "Duke of Earl," a tribute to his extensive wardrobe and the elegant style with which he wore it. Some of the older Tigers felt that it was "too flashy, Hollywood stuff." But even in those years, when most teams, including the Tigers, required their players to wear coats and ties on the road, Wilson's attire was impressive if not somewhat conservative with a decided emphasis on double-breasted suits and striped ties.

Still, the Tigers franchise remained ambivalent about minorities. Many in the organization felt that three was just about the right number of black players (although a fourth would be added later in the season with relief pitcher John Wyatt). Some executives spoke privately about how Hispanic players wilted under pressure. They made sure that there was no chance of that happening with the Tigers. The only Hispanic on the ball club was Julio Moreno, a sad-visaged Cuban who had pitched briefly with Washington in the early '50s. He pitched batting practice, a very low-pressure position.

When Charlie Dressen managed the team he regularly reminded his players that the National League was far tougher. He attributed that to the greater number of blacks in that circuit. Dressen felt they played the game to the hilt and made it faster and meaner. He imported several players from the Dodgers during his tenure in Detroit in an effort to "toughen up" the Tigers. None of them, however, were black.

The Cardinals, on the other hand, fielded a lineup that was predominantly black and Hispanic on the days when Gibson pitched. The Dodgers had also won championships with teams with a large number of minorities. But baseball overall did not regard the career of Dr. King as having any special resonance. The game, after all, had removed its racial bar twenty-two years ago, long before King's entry into the civil rights movement. Black stars were now firmly established. Segregated facilities were a thing of the past. The game had desegregated outposts in Houston and Atlanta. Many baseball men understood the injustice of Jim Crow and King's campaign against it. Some may have even supported it. It just didn't seem to have much to do with them.

On the day after the assassination, Coretta Scott King took her slain husband's place at the head of a Memphis march. It had been scheduled as a show of support for striking garbage workers, but the assassination turned it into a tribute to King. Following the assassination, riots had broken out in Washington, D.C., Chicago, and one hundred other cities. Detroit, still exhausted from the previous summer's violence, remained quiet. In Florida, there had been some disturbances a few miles from Al Lang Field in St. Petersburg. But it was decided that the final exhibition games of the spring would go on as scheduled.

The Cards won the first one, 3–2. Gibson pitched four innings, gave up a run, retired the last eight men in a row, and struck out three. The next day the Tigers won, 4–2. McLain looked unimpressive in three innings. But two rookies, Daryl Patterson and Jon Warden, shut down the St. Louis lineup without a hit for the last three. It was generally supposed that these two teams had a rendezvous in six months to open the World Series at Busch Stadium. So when Kaline crashed a two-run homer in the seventh to win the second game, there was a little bit more enthusiasm in the Detroit dugout than was the standard for a mere exhibition.

Mayo Smith liked what he saw in Patterson and Warden. He sat down to make his final cuts of the spring that night, and the two rookies were kept on the team. He also did a strange thing in the last exhibition game. He brought in Stanley to play a few innings at third base. The center fielder was regarded as the most talented athlete on the team and frequently took a turn fielding grounders during infield drill. Still, actually playing him in the infield seemed like an odd move. It was simply noted as a curiosity, however, and passed over.

As the Tigers flew back to Detroit to start the season, President Johnson proclaimed a national day of mourning for King. All openers scheduled for April 9 were postponed in deference to the funeral service, which was led by King's father at Atlanta's Ebenezer Baptist Church. A mourning nation watched on television as King's coffin, pulled on a wagon by two Georgia mules, was carried to its resting place. Schools shut down. The New York Stock Exchange closed. The Academy Award presentations were rescheduled.

The Tigers, however, were unable to watch the service. Although the opener had been cancelled, the ball club scheduled a team practice for that morning. Wilson was furious. He showed up for the mandatory practice but merely went through the motions. Afterward, he angrily berated team management for what he said was a blatant disregard of the mood of its black players. For once, the world outside seemed to have punctured baseball's cocoon.

CHAPTER 6

The Duke
of Earl

"Did I seem to be angry? Well, maybe I was. Part of it was, you know, maybe a defensive thing towards the media. But I'd lived through a lot of things to be angry about, too."

Earl Wilson pitched his last ball game in 1970, just two years after catching the only winner of his eleven-year big league career. He then walked away from baseball and never looked back. His office in the small auto-supplier factory he owns in the Detroit suburb of Farmington Hills is devoid of any baseball memorabilia. He prefers it that way.

"Baseball belongs to another life," he says in the comfortable reception area outside his private office. "Don't get me wrong. It was a good life. But there's no comparison in my mind. There is nothing I experienced in baseball that compares to the excitement of handing out your payroll checks . . . and then driving like hell to the bank to make sure that they're covered. Now that's excitement."

Wilson laughs heartily as he makes the comparison. In his

mid-fifties, he is still a handsome man, only a little thicker around the middle than he was as a player. But he has shed a lot of weight, too—most of it in anger.

"You sometimes had to walk softly around the Duke," recalls Gates Brown with a small smile.

Wilson's explosions were legendary in the Detroit clubhouse. Teammates and reporters alike could never tell when one was coming. A seemingly innocuous question could prompt a furious, obscene outburst. He might apologize later, throw an arm around your shoulder, and laugh about it. But Wilson's bursts of anger were awesome to behold.

On one occasion, an admirer had shipped him some fresh plums and berries. Wilson had eaten some of them and stowed the rest of the package in his locker to be disposed of later. While he was on the field, some prankish Tigers—to this day no one will confess to it—swiped the package and passed out the goodies around the clubhouse. When Wilson returned and found the empty package, he went ballistic. A practical joke suddenly turned into a roaring confrontation as Wilson stalked around the clubhouse, demanding to know who had stolen his plums. To some of the more cinematic Tigers, it was reminiscent of Captain Queeg raging about his stolen strawberries in *The Caine Mutiny*. But Wilson was a lot bigger and angrier than Humphrey Bogart had been in that role.

"I've got to admit I don't recall much about that incident," he says. "Which isn't to say it didn't happen. It's just been a long, long time, and my mind is on so many other things.

"But, yes, I was an angry man. I was the only African-American on that team who'd grown up in the South. Louisiana. You don't forget the things you saw when you were a kid. The thing is when I was that age and actually going through it, it didn't seem so bad to me. Only when I got a little older and started looking back did I realize how awful it was. I got to understand there were parts of life that I had never even explored because they were closed to me.

"My family moved to San Diego when I was a teenager, and I

finished growing up out there. But when I signed with the Red Sox, they sent me right back into it. Playing in Montgomery, Alabama, in the late 1950s. No fun.

"But, you know, black folks are so precious to me. We'd be on these bus trips, and the team would stop for food at some dump on the highway. The black players couldn't get off the bus and go inside. But the black people who worked in these places always made sure that we got something good. These old ladies would come running out to the bus with a meal thay had fixed special for us. We probably ate better than the white players did. They were inside eating hamburgers, and we were getting some good food back on the bus. And they never let us pay for a thing.

"Even when I got to the big club, though, it didn't end. The black players with the Red Sox were routinely refused service in Florida. I even walked into the general manager's office and demanded a trade to a team that trained in Arizona. You can't know how degrading that was. It was baseball's dirty secret back then.

"I still remember clearly coming into Detroit for the first time with Boston. It was the first time I had ever been in a city where black people were in the middle class. They had their own homes, new cars, livin' the life. They took me to this neighborhood of huge old homes, mansions, big trees—Arden Park, I think it was—and told me that most of the houses were owned by blacks. I couldn't believe it. I fell in love with this city right then. I told myself that this is where I wanted to live when my career was over. I never could have guessed it'd happen the way it did, though."

Wilson came to the Tigers in June 1966 in a trade for outfielder Don Demeter—one of the ex-Dodgers whom Dressen had thought would toughen up the team. That hadn't worked out because Demeter had become a devout Christian, as mild a man as one ever saw in the majors. Dressen was deeply disappointed. But Wilson quickly stepped into the starting rotation, the only member of that group who hadn't come through the Detroit system. Then in 1967 he won twenty-two games, tying for the league lead in that stat. He also changed mentally. Under

Freehan's constant prodding, Wilson became a finisher. In his previous five years with Boston he completed only twenty-five games. In just two seasons with Detroit, he matched that total. He was the automatic choice to pitch the 1968 season opener against Boston.

"I remember that workout on the day of Dr. King's funeral," Wilson says. "Since I was pitching the next day there wasn't much I was going to do anyhow. But everyone had to be there. Then they announced that same day about how the entire team had to show up for this charity event for the Capuchin Soup Kitchen. This was one of the Tigers' favorite charities, an annual thing. Attendance was always mandatory. But this year they announced they were moving it to the suburbs, some big banquet hall out in Southfield. I guess it was the riots or something, and white people still didn't want to come downtown.

"I can't change who I am. If you don't want to hear what I have to say, don't ask me. That went from Jim Campbell to the batboy. Don't tell me how I should be living my life. Did that mean I had a chip on my shoulder? Well, in my mind right's right and wrong's wrong. The death of Dr. King was still on my mind. Then when I heard about where they were moving this dinner the first thought I had was that there weren't going to be any little black kids there. So I went to Willie and to Gates and said, 'Let's not go.' I knew it wouldn't come out right in the media. And we did have our butts handed to us when the story got out. But you know what? They made sure that there were black kids at that event, and that's what was important.

"What I remember about the opener in '68 was that I didn't do too well. I was gone by the sixth, and they beat us, 7–3. Carl Yastrzemski hit two home runs, but not off me, and everyone was wondering if it was going to be just like last year, with Yaz killing us. What I do remember was that my first time up I hit a home run. I prided myself on my hitting. To me it was another weapon I had as a pitcher. It infuriated me when they brought in the designated hitter. That came in after I retired, but they started talking about it back then. That penalized pitchers like me who worked on their hitting, who cared enough about it to make themselves good at it. I hit thirty-five home runs in my career. The fans used to love to watch me hit because they knew it wasn't automatic. I could hit one out anytime. If I pitched for the Tigers today I'd never even come to the plate.

"I bet you didn't know I was the first big league player to have an agent. It's true. I hired Bob Woolf from Boston to do my negotiating. But it was all in secret. They wouldn't even talk to agents back then. They weren't allowed in baseball. So when I went in to talk to Campbell, he'd make an offer and I'd get up and excuse myself to go to the bathroom. Then I'd run down the hall and call Woolf on the phone, and he'd tell me what to say. Campbell must have thought my bladder had shrunk or something. I don't know how much more I made because of Woolf but I think it was a few thousand—not bad money back then. When I told Campbell about it years later he told me: 'Earl, I suspected something was up because you're not that goddamned smart.' But I thought Jim was a fair man. I respected him, and now that I run a company and see it all from the other side. I appreciate what he did, too."

Wilson gets up and insists on taking his visitor on a tour of his 60,000-square-foot operation, situated in a sprawling industrial park. It is called Auto-Tek and manufactures the insulation that protects various small parts within a car. The sign at the front office window reads: "Appointments only; 30 minutes maximum time available. E.W." The business is doing well.

"Maybe I didn't achieve as much as I should have as a player," says Wilson. "And maybe I achieved more than I should have in business. I'll take that tradeoff. This is like a ball club, though. Give me what I need, and I'll play you. Sure, I make a special effort to hire minorities here. I feel that's my obligation. But I tell them, look, I bust my ass for this business to survive, and I expect the same from you. If you can't give me that, I don't want you here. Because my first obligation is to my company."

The tour is over, and Wilson, smiling and at ease, says his goodbyes.

"What I remember about that team in 1968," he says, "is that there were no divisions. We were all like brothers. People don't ever get comfortable with each other when race gets into it. But for that one year, at least, that wasn't the case. We were really together.

"I don't do the card shows or autograph things. But almost every day someone comes up to me and wants to talk about that season. Little kids who couldn't have been born until twenty-five years later. They know the legacy. I get grown men who come up to me with a baseball or a scorecard I had signed for them back then, and they tell me how much it meant to them. It's like I'm revered. Man, I get chills. What did I do? All I did was play a game."

CHAPTER 7

April
Getaway

The sense of deja vu thickened in the season's second game. With Lolich on National Guard duty because of lingering unrest after the King assassination, McLain was given the start. He had the Red Sox shut out, 3–0, on three hits into the sixth. Then a single and consecutive home runs tied the score. This came the day after Yaz had hit two out of the park in the opener. The Tigers had seen this script before and hadn't liked it the first time around.

But Warden, the rookie left-hander who made the roster on the last day of spring training, stopped Boston over the last two innings. He was scheduled to be the first hitter in the last of the ninth. Mayo sent up Gates Brown instead.

It was Brown's first appearance of the season. He had dislocated his wrist the previous year and got to bat just ninety-one times, hitting a wretched .187. It was far and away his worst season in the majors. Detroit reportedly had tried to deal him off during the winter only to find no interest. He made the roster only by the slimmest of margins. Mayo did not care much for his defensive skills ("There are times you wonder if the guy can throw the ball across the street," he said on one occasion). If he couldn't hit, the manager felt, he was useless. Brown was the last left-handed batter remaining on the bench when he got the call from Mayo.

Gates was facing John Wyatt, Boston's top reliever a closer before anyone ever thought to use that word. Wyatt was suspected of throwing a Vaseline ball, loading it up with dabs of petroleum jelly hidden somewhere on his person. The stuff made his fastball collapse downward in a nasty and illegal manner just as it reached the plate. Wyatt encouraged speculation about this secret weapon. When he joined the Tigers later in the summer, a jar of Vaseline was displayed like a trophy in a place of honor in his locker.

But whatever jelly Wyatt was spreading in this game, Gates used it for a sandwich. He rifled Wyatt's delivery into the right field upper deck. The Tigers were winners for the first time that year.

Chicago came in and lost twice. Then the Tigers went to Fenway, where they ruined Boston's home opener with a win. Then back home to beat Cleveland twice and finally on to Chicago, where they won three more from the White Sox. It was nine in a row for Detroit since the opening day loss. On April 21, after the first game in Chicago, they went into first place alone. They would be out of it only six days the rest of the season.

The interesting thing about this spurt was that five of the nine wins were accumulated by the bull pen, with Warden getting three of them. It seemed that Mayo's prescription for strengthening the relief staff had worked. Moreover, four of the games, including the one Gates ended, rolled home on the last time at bat. The most dramatic was Horton's two-out, two-run shot in the tenth that beat Cleveland, 4–3. The two top pitchers from the previous season, Wilson and Sparma, were also off to good starts. Wilson won twice, while Sparma fired a shutout at the Indians. During the streak, the Tigers staff gave up only eighteen runs.

McLain finally got on the win list in his third start, notching the ninth game in the streak with a workmanlike 4–2 stifling of the White Sox. Denny took special delight in beating Chicago. It was his hometown team. He had signed with Chicago at eighteen, right out of prep school at Mt. Carmel High, where he was a 38–7 sensation during his career. But the Sox were overstocked with young right-handers in the spring of 1963. Their top prospect was Dave DeBusschere, a six-foot-six intimidator who would soon decide that banging away as a power forward with the Detroit Pistons suited him better than pitching. McLain was matched against the third prospect, Bruce Howard, in an intrasquad game. When Howard won, McLain was cut from the big league roster. The Tigers quickly snapped him up in the first-year draft. He went 18–6 in the minors and by the end of that season was pitching for Detroit.

Mayo was busily experimenting. He was still intrigued by the idea of getting Stanley into the infield. So whenever the Tigers faced a left-hander he sat down Cash, who had edged out Mathews in the battle for first base, and played Stanley there, with Northrup moving to center. Cash was deeply annoyed. But he was getting used to it.

Northrup recalls, "Every year they would bring in some hotshot who was going to move Norman to the bench. It got to be funny. Here was a guy who hit twenty-five to thirty homers and knocked in eighty-five runs season after season, and they were always getting ready to move him out. Norman used to say the dumbest thing he ever did was hit .361 that one season early in his career. Everyone was always waiting for him to hit like that again, and he just wasn't that kind of hitter. That was 1961, an expansion season. The pitching was down all over the league, and he had Kaline and Rocky Colavito, both having tremendous seasons, hitting around him. It wasn't going to happen like that for him again."

Cash was another ex-member of the White Sox. He had been a utility man on the 1959 pennant winners and then was traded to Cleveland as a throw-in on a major deal. Detroit picked him up at the end of spring training in 1960 for a minor league infielder—a deal that ranked as one of the biggest steals in franchise history. A few days later, the two teams swung a real stunner as Detroit landed home run champ Colavito in exchange for the previous year's batting leader, Harvey Kuenn. Cash and Colavito would combine for 263 home runs over the next four seasons with Detroit.

Cash's failure to repeat his big year disappointed not only his bosses. But it also made him the top target for the frustrations of Detroit's fans. He was booed throughout his career at Tiger Stadium. Cash could look very inadequate against some left-handers. He was also a streak hitter, and when he was going bad, pulling his head off the ball in an effort to reach the cozy right field stands in Detroit, it seemed he couldn't hit anybody. During 1967, as the booing hit new crescendos, he pulled off his cap on one occasion and waved it mockingly at the crowd as he went back to the dugout. It was a rare lapse for a man who seemed to find humor in any situation.

In one game, upon realizing that he had been picked off first base, he raised his hands and signaled hopefully for a time-out. When play was suspended during a rainstorm another time, Cash was on second base. But when the game resumed, he trotted out to third. "What are you doing over there?" he was asked by the umpire. "I stole third," he replied. "When did that happen?" asked the ump, earnestly puzzled. "During the rain," said Norman.

When flamboyant umpire Emmett Ashford ran out to his position, arms outspread, at the start of a game, Cash came running right after him, taking a flying dive off the pitcher's mound with his arms flapping, as if trying to gain altitude. But his most famous exploit was when he tried to come to bat against Nolan Ryan, in the midst of a no-hitter, using a table leg as a bat. "I couldn't hit him with a regular bat so I thought I'd try this," he explained.

Cash was easily the most popular man on the team. He knew where all the best watering holes—the places where people were eager to buy drinks for big league stars—were located in every American League city. A night out with Norman could easily

stretch into positions on the clock that for most people only
came once a day. It was part of Tigers lore that he could show up
at the ballpark looking as haggard and woebegone as Texas road-
kill. Then he would miraculously recover somehow and get two
hits. The other players admired him as a warrior, a man who
would play despite injury, hangover, rain, sleet, and dark of night.
He was a throwback to a long line of ballplayers. The Gas House
Gang, Paul Waner, Babe Ruth—players who never let their love
of liquid refreshment get in the way of a ball game.

Later in the season, when an injury to Kaline necessitated a
permanent return to the outfield for Stanley, Mayo still stuck to
his platooning plan. He started Freehan at first base against
left-handers. Cash ended up playing in just 127 games, his lowest total since his first season in Detroit. While he grumbled
about the play, he kept it low key. He was too good a soldier to
complain loudly when the team was winning. Just once, when
Mayo told him to go in as a late defensive replacement, did he
balk, snapping that he wasn't anybody's caddy. Mayo sent
Mathews in, instead, and nothing more was said. Whatever
other flaws Mayo may have had, he seemed to know when
pushing too hard might damage the cohesiveness that his ball
club had created.

Besides, strange things were happening. "We didn't win games
like these last year," mused Mayo as the winning streak length-
ened. One of the reasons might have been that the Tigers didn't
have Warden before. In the first eight games he ever spent on a big
league roster, the twenty-one-year-old rookie won three of them.

CHAPTER 8

An Easy
Kind of Game

His garage may be full of sneakers, but his head is full of memories.

Almost three decades have passed since sporting goods salesman Jon Warden threw the final pitch of his brief major league career. But the details are as vivid as last summer's vacation. The sounds, the texture of his single season in the sun, come pouring into the house in suburban Cincinnati.

"I am a walking trivia answer," he laughs as he picks his way through the stacked boxes of athletic shoes stored in the garage. No room for the cars. They're out on the driveway. He is wearing a warm-up suit and baseball cap, which hides the few tufts that remain atop his head.

"Who was the only Tiger who didn't get into the 1968 World Series?" Warden raises his hand and guffaws. "That's who I am."

"It all happened so fast. One day, no one knows who I am, fresh up from Double A, and I'm on the roster of the Detroit Tigers, and we're fighting for a pennant. Next day my arm is gone, and my career is over. But I loved every minute of it. Even while it was happening I knew that it was an experience that would last me the rest of my life. To tell you the truth, I'm just grateful that I got to be a part of it."

He was just twenty-one that spring, the last man to make the Tigers roster in Florida. A hard-throwing lefty out of Columbus, Ohio.

"I was hoping to get sent to Toledo, the Triple A team. That way my folks would have been able to drive up and see me play. The big team, I never thought there was any chance. I mean, they had just missed the pennant by a game. What did they want with some young kid who couldn't find his butt with both hands? But they were looking for young arms, and I had one of them.

"They had to cut Hank Aguirre to keep me. Man, that could have been real rough. They could have treated me like dirt. Hank was one of the most popular guys on that team. Everybody loved him. Then one day he's gone and here I am, fresh out of Rocky Mount, with all of two years of pro ball behind me. But you know what? No one ever said a word to me about that. These guys were so dedicated to winning that year that no matter what it took they would accept it. Animosity kind of fell by the wayside. As long as I could help 'em win the thing, I was welcome.

"Poor Hank. He never got to the series. He landed with the Cubs in 1969, and it looked like they were going to breeze in. But then they collapsed down the stretch, of course. The Mets caught 'em, and Hank never got in. For years afterwards, whenever there was a Tigers alumni meeting, he'd come running up to me, grab my hand, and say: 'You sonofabitch, you've got my ring.' He'd laugh about it, but I know sometimes it had to tear him up."

Warden had one of the more remarkable debuts in baseball history. Three appearances, three and one-third innings pitched, three wins.

"Man, I thought this was the easiest game in the world," he says. "Naw. Not really. My locker was right next to Lolich's, and he'd keep telling me, 'Your bubble will break, rookie.' But it took a while, and I was on cloud nine.

"The first man I faced in the big leagues was Reggie Smith. My knees were shaking so hard I could barely stand up on the mound. But he sent a grounder right at Ray Oyler at short, and I took a big, deep breath. That was automatic. And then Oyler booted the ball, and I just about died. George Scott got a single and now I've got two men on, nobody out, in a tie game. But I got it together and got Joe Foy on a fly ball for the third out with the bases loaded.

"Then there's two out in the ninth, and up comes Yastrzemski. Oh, man. I'm shaking all over again. I just turned that ball loose with everything I had, and I struck him out. My first major league strikeout, and it's Yaz. I can't believe it. I'm sitting on the bench, turning that over in my mind, and I look up and Gates Brown hits the ball out of the park. I'm the winning pitcher. This was crazy. Everything was happening at once.

"Three games later, Mayo brings me in again. It's the tenth, and Cleveland has just gone ahead of us with one out. I get Jose Vidal on a fly ball and start thinking about Duke Sims when Jose Cardenal tries to steal second, and Freehan throws him out. So I'm out of that pretty easy. We come up, Horton busts a two-run homer, and I win again.

"All right, I'm really enjoying this. Now we're in Chicago. We've got a 1–0 lead in the ninth, bases loaded, one out, and here comes the signal for me again. Wayne Causey is the hitter, and I couldn't come anywhere near the plate. I walk him and force in a run, and now Chicago brings up Ken Boyer to bat. By this time he was near the end of his career. But, still. Ken Boyer! I'm waiting for Mayo to make the move and get me out of there. But he never leaves the dugout. I don't know. We all know Mayo wasn't some kind of managerial genius. Sometimes he did strange things. I guess this was just one of them.

"Boyer scorches one. I mean it's a rocket. But it's right at Don Wert. He stabs it, steps on third, double play, end of the inning. The guys score three times in the top of the tenth, and I win again."

It didn't end there. Not quite. Warden got into twenty-five

more games for the Tigers. He won one, and he lost one. When it came time to pick the series roster it was between him and John Wyatt. Mayo, looking for another lefty, went with Warden, but never used him. He had pitched his last game for the Tigers and, as it turned out, in the majors.

"Kansas City picked me in the expansion draft that fall," he says. "That was real funny. It was like a week after the series was over. One day I'm celebrating a world championship, and the next day I'm gone. I'm not a part of it anymore. It wasn't unexpected but still I kept hoping they'd pick somebody else.

"It was a great opportunity, being on an expansion team. They told us the first day of spring training that every job was wide open. So I went right out and threw my arm out. Rotator cuff. Even now that's a tough deal, but in 1969 it was a career-ender. I tried it in the minors for a while, and the Royals did bring me up to the big club at the end of the season. So technically I did get back to the majors, even though I was never in a game. But after the season, I got cut, and that was that."

As he spoke, Warden had just returned from a big league alumni golf tournament in Florida. He is active in the group and seldom misses a chance to attend meetings in his area.

"The first thing we have to instill in the new members is that now it's different," he says. "Now we want you to sign autographs. You don't give fans the brush-off. Man, some of the attitudes these guys have today. You got to give 'em a makeover.

"I look back on that season, and the thing I remember most is the other guys. Rooming with McLain. Now that was an experience. It was just me and an empty bed most of the time. But the rest of us, we'd be playing cards, talking, go out and have a few beers. I guess most of the guys playing ball today make so much money that they don't have to have a roommate. They don't know what they're missing. Even all these years later, you see one of the guys you roomed with, and it's, 'How ya' doin', rooms?' Like no time at all had passed. That was such a big part of the experience.

"Now that I'm in the alumni, I get to know the guys who were big stars. I remember going up to Ernie Banks the first time and telling him how much I admired him and him holding up my ring and saying, 'Yeah, but you got one of these.'

"You know, it doesn't seem to matter whether you made the Hall of Fame or whether you lasted one season, like me. Once a big leaguer, always a big leaguer. If you put the uniform on, it's all the same now."

CHAPTER 9

Stop the
Presses

Something was wrong. The Tigers were cruising in first place as April ended. But it didn't feel right. The city was still hesitant to come out and see them. There were 12,000 empty seats at the opener, a game that traditionally is a sellout in Detroit. Although the Tigers never expect big crowds until Memorial Day and the onset of warmer weather in Michigan, the early turnouts for a first-place team were disappointing. Two-game series with Chicago, Cleveland, and Oakland drew fewer than 20,000 fans each. The Tigers came back from a successful road trip and opened a set against Baltimore, always a good draw. But only 18,000 showed up.

Something was wrong. Only in three seasons since the end of World War II had the Tigers failed to draw one million fans. Attendance peaked in 1950 when the team made a serious run at the Yankees and attracted 1,951,474 customers, the franchise record. In 1961, another contending year, the attendance had been 1.6 million. If not for the riots, that level might have been equalled in 1967. But the final figure was only 1,447,143. With fear still pervasive in the city, some doubted that total attendance would get even that high in 1968, no matter what the team did.

Detroit was still a great baseball city. But it was a city that had lost its center. Its sense of community lay shattered in the spring of 1968, just as thoroughly as the shop windows on 12th Street. Most of the debris from the July riots had been cleared. There were plans to remake 12th Street into a parklike boulevard, to sweep away any memory of what had happened there. Several committees were put together, made up of the town's heavy hitters—automotive executives, union officials, prominent black leaders. They gave themselves hopeful names, like Detroit Renaissance, and tried to work out a plan for restoration. They listened to complaints that had long been ignored. But they had trouble coming to terms with what had happened.

As Earl Wilson had observed on his first visit to Detroit, this was a city with a large, prosperous black middle class. Only Washington, D.C., with its base of government workers, had a higher average income in its black community. Detroit's wealth came out of the auto plants. Those jobs paid better than any other industrial work in the country, and the United Auto Workers was a leader in promoting equal opportunity for blacks. The restrictive housing covenants that had kept the city's swelling black community penned up around Paradise Valley, on the East Side, had been struck down after the war. Blacks were now served in downtown restaurants, employed at the huge J. L. Hudson's department store on Woodward Avenue. Although the farthest reaches of the city, where the best schools were located, were still virtually all-white, a small flow of black families was moving into those neighborhoods.

Sociologists called it a revolution of rising expectations. People scrambling for the bare necessities of life did not start riots. It was among those who felt that they should be getting more, who had gained a toehold and now wanted the whole leg, that discontent was highest. The city had prided itself on its progressive policies. It had welcomed Martin Luther King to town in

1963. He led a march down Woodward, giving an early version of the "I have a dream" speech that he would deliver, memorably, later that summer at the Lincoln Memorial. While other cities went up in flames in the '60s—Cleveland and Los Angeles and Newark—Detroit assured itself smugly that that would never happen there. Now the city could not recover from the shock. Whites behaved as if they had been betrayed, and black rhetoric reached new heights of threats and indignation.

Rumors swirled everywhere. Reports of new armed insurrections. Riot deaths that the police had concealed. Secret prisons being built for black leaders. You heard the rumors wherever you went in the spring of 1968. There was no reality check on the rumors, either, because both of the city's daily newspapers were shut down, their employees locked out since the previous November in a labor dispute.

Even now, it is one of the aspects of the pennant year that many of the Tigers bring up. There were no newspapers, and that took the pressure off. Only later did the players realize that there would also be no stories to clip and paste in scrapbooks to show their grandchildren, no way to build up early fan enthusiasm.

In the late '60s, technology did not allow television to give the extensive game coverage that goes on today. No videotape, no minicams. Equipment was bulky, processing was slow. Radio was still predominantly an entertainment medium, with news and sports coverage as an afterthought. All-news radio and talk radio were still a decade away. The wire services covered the team, but their stories ran in papers far away and went unread by the Tigers. Reporters from a few suburban dailies came to home games but never went on the road. There was even a writer from the Polish-language daily assigned to the team. And when the Communist Party decided that Detroit's masses might welcome some dialectic with their baseball coverage, the communist *Daily World* also sent a reporter to do spot stories. He didn't understand much about the game and was inclined to write sentences like "Norm Cash really rattled the old drainpipes last week." Needless to say, neither the *Dziennik Polski* nor the *Daily World* had much of a readership among the players. To them, the newspaper lockout was liberating.

When compared with the tone of coverage in places like Boston or New York, however, Detroit's sportswriters were mild. Rarely did they agitate for the sheer hell of it, like the Boston writers who had driven the young Ted Williams wild. Seldom did they resort to ridicule, like the New York writers who called themselves "the Chipmunks." But the two top sports columnists in Detroit, Joe Falls at the *Free Press* and Pete Waldmeir at the *News*, were tough. They were truth-tellers, serious and exceptionally talented reporters. Their writing was consistently sharp-edged and irreverent. They did not believe either in leading cheers for the home team or in taunting the opposition.

Falls, a rather puckish man with the accent of his native Queens evident in every syllable he spoke, had been a baseball writer for more than ten years. His sources within the Tigers organization and throughout the game were superb. One of his more memorable features had run the day after Mickey Mantle hammered a tremendous home run over the right field roof at Tiger Stadium. Under the headline "Detroit's New Mantle Shift," Falls's paper ran a photo of Kaline in fielding position atop the roof. People in the Tigers front office went wild, accusing Falls of endangering the life of their best player. Falls had to reassure them that the photo was a gag, a pasteup of Kaline superimposed on the roof. They still didn't think it was funny.

Waldmeir, who would soon become a top political columnist, had grown up on the city's East Side and joined the sports staff while still in college. He was the more ascerbic of the two. While interviewing McLain, the pitcher had made a most unlikely statement, then added, "And may God strike me down if that isn't the truth." Waldmeir took that and ran with it, constructing a wild scenario about panic-stricken Tigers scampering off in terror whenever McLain stood up to speak. The Tigers didn't think that was very funny, either.

At any given moment, a half dozen players were not on speaking terms with either columnist. But that was all right because neither had much to say to the other, either. They disliked one another acutely, an attitude that arose naturally in this hotly competitive newspaper city. The two baseball beat writers rarely spoke to each other, either. When Waldmeir was observed by his paper's beat writer having breakfast with the rival beat writer, Waldmeir said ruefully: "I think I'd rather have my wife catch me in bed with another woman than what just happened."

So the players had some reason to chortle over the writers' absence. But the lack of newspapers compounded the sense of unease in the city. Detroit was flying blind, and it was regarded as unwise to venture too far from home.

Diehards still managed to find their way to the city's premier gathering place for the sports crowd. The Lindell A. C., a ten-minute walk from the ballpark along Michigan Avenue, was the undisputed holder of that title. There were no sports bars in 1968, no strategically raised television sets beaming an endless assortment of games from the cable networks or satellite dish. The Lindell was just a place where players and fans could hang out. All four of the city's professional teams played a short distance away, and fans soon realized that if they went in after a game they might have a chance to share a beer with their heroes. Even the visiting teams knew about it and frequented the Lindell.

The name of the place was a joke, an excuse a customer had used when the saloon was in a former location. He had phoned his wife and told her that he had stopped in at his athletic club on the way home. But the Lindell achieved everlasting fame in 1963. The star tackle of the Detroit Lions, Alex Karras, then under a year's suspension for gambling, had signed up for a wrestling match against Dick the Bruiser. The Lindell was a favorite spot for Karras because the owners of the place, the Butsicaris brothers, were also of Greek descent. It was arranged for Karras and the Bruiser to encounter one another there in a scripted meeting to hype the bout. Then someone tossed away the script. The two men were soon flailing away in a genuine chair-throwing, window-smashing brawl that had to be quelled by the quelling squad from the First Precinct. Later on, the Lindell's pugilistic reputation would be further enhanced. Billy Martin, who was then managing the Twins, chose its parking lot as the place to cold-cock his star pitcher, Dave Boswell, to settle a difference of opinion.

The Lindell served up enormous burgers and had in its trophy case one of the city's most cherished exhibits—the jock strap formerly worn by All-Pro Lions linebacker Wayne Walker. Everybody in sports went to the Lindell, except for the lordly Yankees, who preferred a quieter, Manhattanish spot two blocks away called Danny's Gin Mill. But even at the Lindell the season was starting off slowly, much too quietly for a first-place team. It was as if everyone in Detroit was waiting to see what would happen next. Could they dare to hope again about this team and this city?

CHAPTER 10

The Shuffleboard King

When Eddie Mathews joined the Tigers in August of 1967, one of the first things he saw was a message scrawled on a blackboard outside the clubhouse. "Let's win this in spite of Mayo," someone had written. Mathews quickly erased it and sternly lectured his teammates about proper decorum on a contending team. Rule one: You don't blind-side the manager.

That little incident spoke volumes about Mayo, Mathews, and the meaning of leadership on the 1968 Tigers. Mathews, a long-time star with the Braves, stepped naturally into the role. He was respected by all the players, and especially by his peers, Kaline and Cash. He had been there and done that. Mathews performed brilliantly under the greatest pressure imaginable in the 1957 Series, when the Milwaukee Braves, the team from Bushville, upended the haughty Yankees. Ballplayers respected that. They knew a little history. So even though he was only a shadow of the player he once had been, Mathews quickly became a respected voice in the clubhouse. He knew how to win, and the Tigers were eager to learn.

There were several leaders on this ball club. But Kaline led by example rather than overtly, and Cash was too quick to find the humor in a situation to take himself seriously as a leader. The position fell to the newcomer, Mathews.

This was not a team with a great deal of respect for the man who was its nominal leader. Mayo Smith was named manager after a calamitous 1966 season. He was not regarded as a pick out of left field. That would have been too close. It was more like a pick out of the hospitality room. Mayo carried the nickname "America's Guest." He was a fixture in baseball, a familiar figure before and after games in the room where free food and drink were served to club officials and media. A handsome man with a head full of gray hair. A dapper dresser who savored a glass of good bourbon. A man with the knack of making you feel that you were one of the wittiest and most perceptive individuals he had ever met . . . even if he hadn't quite caught your name or knew what you were talking about.

He was also modest in appraising his own abilities. After the World Series, upon a triumphant return to his home in Lake Worth, Florida, he was given a parade. While walking to his official car, he claimed, he heard two elderly ladies talking about the event. "What's the big deal?" one of them demanded. "Why, haven't you heard?" her friend replied. "The shuffleboard king is back in town."

The announcement that Mayo would manage the Tigers was met with whoops of derision. The city was expecting a firebrand, someone to whip the team into contention. "America's Guest" wasn't quite what Tiger fans or media had pictured. But it wasn't as if he hadn't paid his dues. He had, three times over. Mayo had played seventeen years in the minor leagues, reaching the bigs only as a wartime fill-in with the 1945 As. He hit .212. That part was all right. Several successful managers never spent a day in the majors. But Mayo's record was not too good as a manager, either. In parts of five seasons with the Phillies and Reds, he never finished above .500. Moreover, his last managing job had expired in 1959. Fred Hutchinson replaced him, took a team that was in seventh place under Mayo, and in less than two years won a pennant. Had the Tigers gone nuts hiring this guy?

Actually, the hiring of Mayo was the result of deliberate consideration by general manager Jim Campbell and his top advisor, Rick Ferrell. The team had been stunned in 1966 by the deaths of two managers. Charlie Dressen, who had been brought in to mold the young players into a contender, suffered a heart attack in June and died two months later. He was replaced by veteran coach Bob Swift, who developed cancer and passed away in October. The Tigers finished the year under the guidance of another coach, Frank Skaff. It was a demoralizing, tumultuous experience.

Dressen, for all his peculiarities, his mangling of the English language, and his serene conviction that he was a genius, had done his job well. He had brought along the Boys from Syracuse steadily, making sure they had a chance to taste success in equal measure with failure. The veterans liked him. To Willie Horton, who had lost his parents in a car crash on the eve of stardom, Dressen was a surrogate father. The death of Dressen and the subsequent death of Swift were devastating blows to the young team.

What the Tigers needed more than anything else was a calming presence. Enter Mayo Smith. He was so calm that he sometimes seemed inert. The players soon started referring to him as "Awww, what the fuck," because that seemed to be his response to virtually every event, good or bad. McLain, who had been a favorite of Dressen, tried to ingratiate himself with the new manager early in his term by parading around the clubhouse after a late-inning win and saying, "At last we've got a manager in here." Mayo wasn't buying any of that. "Mickey Mouse makes those moves," he said privately. It also warned him that some players would bear watching.

He had made one inspired change, shifting McAuliffe from shortstop to second base. In one move he had acquired an outstanding second baseman and lost a mediocre shortstop. He then handed the shortstop job to Oyler, who never dropped anything except his bat. Mayo had blown up at the team just once, over what he regarded as indifferent play at the start of an important series in Boston in 1967. He closed the clubhouse doors and, red-faced, let his players have it full bore. Some Tigers, most notably Freehan, wished he would have done that more often. This was a team that sometimes required a shaking-up. But that wasn't Mayo's style.

Eventually, some of the players began to question his decisions, his handling of the bench and the bull pen down the stretch in '67. Mayo himself did not regard his talents as lying in the realm of tactics.

"Most of the stuff you do on the field is dictated by events," he said. "That's not the managing part. It's the twenty-five guys. Knowing how to handle each one. Who needs a word and who needs a kick in the ass. That's the part."

Making his job even more difficult was his pitching coach. John Sain had been hired along with Mayo and was the best in the business. But he had his peculiarities. He insisted on bringing along his own bull pen coach, Hal Naragon. He also insisted on being given free rein with the pitchers. Sain had many theories about pitching. He believed that it was essentially mental. Before attaining success, you had to visualize yourself as successful. That was half the battle. He gave out subscriptions to the magazine *Success Unlimited* as Christmas presents. He also encouraged his pitchers to be secretive, not to share information with anyone. When McLain did a magazine photo spread on the grips he used to throw various pitches, on Sain's advice he simply made them up on the spot. He even demonstrated how he gripped pitches he never threw.

Sain liked his pitchers seated in a separate part of the clubhouse, away from the hitting riffraff. He even lived off by himself, in a motel near the airport. But he stopped short of demanding that his pitchers do that, too.

It all seemed to be effective. In two years, the staff earned run average had fallen from the second worst in the league (3.85) to the third best (2.71.) What wasn't generally noticed at the time was that the league ERA had gone down by 0.46 over the same period to a historic low of 2.98 in 1968. It was a season thoroughly dominated by pitchers. But Sain earned a lot of the credit in Detroit.

Mayo took it all in, seeing more than anyone guessed. He understood the problems that McLain and Sain were causing. He also knew that the team was winning and was willing to let it ride. He had come too far, waited too long to board this train. He wasn't about to drive it off the tracks.

CHAPTER 11

The Rivals

Whatever the manager's opinion of McLain, it quickly became evident that his was going to be no ordinary season. He reeled off five straight wins, all complete games. The fifth one, a 12–1 crushing of Washington on May 10, put the Tigers in first place for keeps. He lasted just two innings in his next start against Baltimore. But in the following thirteen assignments, up to the All-Star Game break on July 7, McLain would go 11–1. His overall record was then 16–2. He was poised to do something absolutely remarkable.

It was also evident that he would not do it quietly. McLain was temperamentally incapable of that. Two years before, for no apparent reason, he tried to talk himself into a feud with Sam McDowell, acknowledged to be the hardest thrower in the league. McLain called him immature, dumb, and incapable of harnessing his abilities. Only when his remarks reached print did it occur to McLain that Sudden Sam might not see the humor in the situation. That he might, in fact, try to enlarge McLain's ear canal when next they met. So he backed off that story quickly. McDowell's comment on the whole episode was: "Goo goo, da, da," which may have been a fairly accurate assessment.

But still McLain would have his say. He always had a surprise or two for inquiring minds. He loved Pepsi, even kept a glass of it on his night table so he could take a swig of it, lukewarm, as soon as he awoke in the morning. He considered himself a serious musician, an organist who happened to play baseball rather than the other way around. He was going to take up flying his own plane, an ambition that won him the nickname "Sky King" among the other Tigers. Understandably, he always drew a cluster of writers around his locker.

In early May, McLain was asked by a wire service reporter to explain why attendance had been so low at Tiger Stadium. "Tiger fans are the biggest front-runners in the world," McLain said. "If they think we're stupid for playing this game, how stupid are they for coming out to watch us?" He continued in this vein for several minutes. His remarks went out on the radio wire and led every sportscast in town the next day. The first crowd of over 20,000 since opening day then turned up at McLain's next start and booed him incessantly from the first pitch. His five-game win streak ended that night. "I only meant some of the fans," McLain said in clarification. He really didn't need the papers to be publishing to get into trouble.

While Denny rolled merrily along, Lolich was off to his usual tepid start. His emergency National Guard duty during the April rioting set back his routine, and he still faced the usual two weeks away during his annual summer training in June. By the time McLain had won his eighth game of the year, Lolich had won just twice, the least of any starter. The Tigers had hoped that his heroic finish in 1967 would carry over into the new season. But the Lolich who started the 1968 campaign was the same pitcher who had struggled through most of the previous year.

"Mickey just didn't have confidence in himself," says Freehan. "He didn't think he could make the big pitches late in the game. There was an element lacking. We all knew that when he was on, there was no one with more stuff. But convincing Mickey of that was a little harder."

Lolich himself seethed silently over McLain. Lolich had reached the majors a few months before Denny in 1963 after a tough, erratic, four-year apprenticeship in the minors. When he finally got to Detroit his professional record was a drab 27-44. Only in his final season, pitching with his hometown team in Portland, Oregon, did he have a winning record. He explained later that the left field fence was so close in that park that he had to concentrate on control. That transformed him into a pitcher. In 1964, his first full year with Detroit, he blossomed, going 18–9, and at twenty-three becoming the top pitcher on the staff.

The coming of McLain altered the equation. Although the two gave the Tigers the best young pitching combination in the game, their relationship cut much deeper than a rivalry. McLain's cockiness, which readily translated into arrogance, and his Chicago wise-guy demeanor irritated the daylights out of Lolich, with his conservative Oregon upbringing.

While McLain exuded confidence, Lolich searched for the formula and brooded about what he regarded as a lack of respect for his achievements. After all, with McLain among the missing, Lolich had almost pitched Detroit to the 1967 pennant. But as he struggled again, that all seemed to be forgotten by Mayo and the front office.

The game of May 18 was no help to Lolich's mental state. Frank Howard came into Detroit with the Washington Senators on a home-run binge. He had hit seven in his previous four games, a record, then added one more off Sparma on Friday night. It was Lolich's turn on Saturday. Howard, the biggest man in the game at six-foot-seven and 255 pounds, looked absolutely terrifying when he went off on one of his tears. No one could hit the ball farther and with more force. He was in the first of three straight forty-home-run seasons, emerging, after several rather ordinary years, as the top slugger in the league.

Howard made it nine homers in six games with a wrong-field shot off Lolich in the third. He came up again two innings later with two runners on base. The ball he hit scraped the edge of the left field roof, directly above the foul pole, as it disappeared from sight and landed in the street beyond. Only one other hitter, Harmon Killebrew, ever had cleared the roof in left. The blast was immediately recognized as one of the longest home runs in stadium history, traveling an estimated three and a half miles. The monumental clout gave Lolich another loss, another fracture in his thinning wall of confidence.

The next day, however, the fans showed up. The first Sunday doubleheader of the year brought in 45,491 of them, the biggest home crowd yet. Sunday was still a traditional doubleheader day in 1968. The players hated playing two and, eventually, their union managed to get them eliminated. But this season there were eight on the schedule. Rainouts and suspended games would account for several more, and they usually drew big crowds. With the average game still played in under two and a half hours, twin bills did not turn into endurance contests for players and spectators alike.

Most teams didn't start night games until 8:00 P.M. But as the games grew longer throughout the '70s and '80s, starting times were gradually moved up by an hour or more in most cities. It was the only way that fans could get home before David Letterman signed off. Baseball was played at a far brisker pace in 1968, with even the most critical games rarely going longer than two hours and forty minutes. The reason? There are dozens of theories. Fewer pitching changes. Fewer at-bats that went deep into the count. The wait between half innings was thirty seconds shorter. No designated hitter, which meant fewer runs being scored. All these later contributed to the lengthening of what was intended as a diversion of a few hours and became instead a lumbering affair of Wagnerian duration.

This was also the final season of the winner-take-all pennant race. Or, as the players refer to it now, the last "real" pennant race. No divisions, no playoffs. At the end of 162 games, the top two teams played, and that was it. In close races, it made September meetings between contenders some of the most memorable and excruciating ball games ever played. Because there were no second chances. It would not happen that way after 1968. With both leagues adding two teams the following year, the only instance in which expansion was so closely coordinated, divisional play had arrived.

One alteration already had been made for this year. The American League didn't arrive on the West Coast until 1961, three years after the National. Then the Los Angeles Angels were created in the first wave of expansion. This season, there was a second California team. Charlie Finley had moved his As from Kansas City to Oakland. The move was welcomed by the players. It was always tough to adjust their body clocks to the two-hour time difference on a short stay in California. (The West Coast players argued that it was even tougher for them to go the other way because of higher humidity in the East and Midwest during the summer months.) With Oakland in the league, teams would usually have an entire week to get adjusted.

There was also a problem. Ever since the Dodgers and Giants moved to California in 1958, players had complained about the glare during day games. Hitters and outfielders said they couldn't pick up the ball until much later than they did in other places. Virtually every World Series on the West Coast had featured one important defensive play in which the outcome was influenced by glare. Other teams had warned the Tigers that it was especially bad at the Coliseum, home of the newly minted Oakland As.

In Detroit's first game there, the problem was just the opposite. A storm hit in the seventh inning, and the game was rained out as a 2–2 tie. Earl Wilson also jammed his foot in a play at first base and would have to miss a few starts. But the next day, the glare hit them right between the eyes. With an awful air of inevitability, the calamity they had hoped to avert was suddenly upon them.

McLain and Lew Krausse were involved in a 0–0 battle. It was a twilight game, and the setting sun seemed to accentuate the brightness in the ballpark. The Tigers had just two hits, one of them by Kaline. He came to bat again with one out in the sixth.

A pitch came inside, and Kaline, picking it up too late, reacted slowly. It caught him on the forearm. The pain was excruciating, and at the end of the inning he had to leave the game. After a night of intense discomfort he flew back to Detroit, underwent X-rays, and was diagnosed with a fracture. He would be out for a minimum of a month, possibly longer.

There could be no worse news. Kaline was the soul of the Tigers, their greatest player for the last thirteen years. When he broke his collarbone on a diving catch against the Yankees in 1962, saving a game in the ninth inning, the team immediately nose-dived from contender to also-ran. "We won the game and lost the season," mourned the winning pitcher, Hank Aguirre. In 1967 Kaline had broken a finger when he accidentally jammed his hand in a bat rack. The injury had taken him out of the line-up for more than a month, and the Tigers struggled to remain in the race. Now their best player was down again, possibly taking the season with him.

No one blamed Krausse, but the team was infuriated by the news. The As and Tigers did not like each other much anyhow. There had been a brawl the previous year. The Tigers were frequently involved in such diversions. There were a lot of big, angry guys on the team, and they did not back down. When Oakland's Jack Aker, who had been a central figure in the previous year's brawl, came in to pitch relief the day after Kaline went down, the fuse was lit. Northrup had been elevated to Kaline's number three spot in the batting order. In the sixth, the same inning in which Kaline had been hit, Northrup got it in the back of the head. He went down, dazed, and when he was able to regain his feet his first move was directly at Aker.

Both teams came racing out of their dugouts. Observers called it one of the nastiest baseball fights they had ever seen. Mathews, a genuinely tough guy, took care of Aker with three right chops to the face. Horton, who had left the game with a minor injury, came running out of the clubhouse whirlpool, half-dressed, to get in on the fun. Mayo tried to tackle Northrup to keep him in the game and was kicked in the ribs for his efforts. As the teams trooped off the field after the fifteen-minute altercation, several Oakland fans seated behind the Detroit dugout began swearing at the Tigers. One of the players grabbed a baseball and fired it into the stands. It struck a middle-aged woman, sitting quietly in the vicinity, above her eye and opened a cut. She later filed a $200,000 lawsuit, and subpoenas were served on several club officials on their next trip into town. No one would say who had thrown the ball. But pitcher Dennis Ribant was discreetly traded, and the Tigers quietly settled the case. Some of the players privately said that it was the hardest pitch Ribant had thrown all year.

Detroit lost the game in extra innings and then did the same thing, by the same 7–6 score, in California the next day. Their lead had shriveled to one-half a game, with three still to play in California before they went home. It seemed as if their brief bubble had burst. A critical injury would turn them into a struggling rabble once more. Instead, the 1968 Tigers were about to soar.

CHAPTER 12

The Fox

"Mayo wanted to bench me that day," recalls Jim Northrup. "I wasn't going too well, and he really was into the righty-lefty thing, so he wanted to sit me down because a left-hander was starting."

Northrup shifts his frame on the pillows that support his back and permits himself a small smile. Of all the '68 Tigers, he seems to have changed the least. All gray then, all gray now. Duke Snider had similar hair coloration when he was also in his twenties. So he was called the Silver Fox. Among the Tigers, Northrup's appellation was shortened to Fox. But there was a vulpine quality to him that went deeper than hair. A sardonic wit that seems to sense instinctively where the vulnerabilities hide. A knowing gaze that sizes things up at a glance. A restless, clever mind. Those also remain undiminished.

The pillows are a new addition, though. He has already had one operation to fuse loosened vertebrae and will probably require another. "Who knows how I got it," he shrugs. "Sliding. Banging into a wall. It's unavoidable when you're an athlete.

"Yeah, Mayo was ready to sit me down. He'd moved me into the number three spot in the order when Kaline went out with the arm injury. The team was in first place, though, and Wally Moses went to him and told him not to break up a winning combination. So he compromised and batted me seventh."

It was June 24, at Cleveland's cavernous lakefront stadium. The Tigers had won just two of their last seven and the manager was getting nervous. He was afraid that finally the month-long absence of Kaline was making itself felt. Cleveland had won the first three games of this series, with Steve Hargan and Luis Tiant blanking the Tigers on successive days. Dick Tracewski finally pulled them out of the skid with an astonishing three-run homer off Sam McDowell. Now there was a make-up game, on a Monday originally scheduled as an off day. The Tigers, still scrambling for hits, would face Mike Paul, a young left-hander who threw very hard.

And very wild. In the first inning, he walked four men around a single to Freehan. That brought up Northrup with the bases loaded. Paul struck him out.

"On a terrible pitch," Northrup says. "Around my ankles. I was really overeager and couldn't lay off."

Paul struck him out again in the third, this time with one man on base. The pitcher had settled down, the Indians had banged McLain around for a couple of runs, and going into the fifth Detroit's lead was a narrow 3–2. But when Paul started off by giving up his seventh walk of the game, manager Alvin Dark wanted no more. He brought in Eddie Fisher, a veteran knuckle-baller. The Tigers quickly loaded the bases on him, but he came back to strike out Wert, who waved futilely at the dancing knuckler. That gave Northrup a second chance. "I was just trying to get that flutterball somewhere, since I hadn't hit anything all day," he says. "Somewhere" turned out to be the empty right-field stands, a grand slam for a 7–2 lead.

By the next inning, Fisher was gone, replaced by Hal Kurtz, who was no improvement. He hit Freehan, Horton doubled, and then he hit Wert. For the third time in the game, Northrup was coming up with every base occupied. Dark went to a gangling left-hander, Billy Rohr. By this time it made no difference to Northrup. He took Rohr deep, too, and for the first time in franchise history, a Tiger had hit two grand slams in the same game.

He hit one again five days later, once more before the season ended, and, finally, his fifth slam of the year in the sixth game of the World Series. After the double whammy, however, radio announcer Ernie Harwell would herald Northrup's every appearance at the plate with the phrase: "It's the Slammer himself." It became one of the tag lines of the season in Detroit and marked Northrup as a man to look to in the clutch.

The homers did more than snap Northrup out of his brief slump. They seemed to be a turning point in his career. Previously, he had hit in the number two position, a place in the lineup where bat control rather than power is essential. For the rest of the season he was a consistent long-ball threat in the three slot. The pressure of replacing the wounded Kaline turned him into a different player. He led the team with ninety RBIs, hit over twenty homers for the first time, and finally fulfilled the promise that he had always shown.

Northrup grew up in the little town of St. Louis, Michigan, a few miles outside of Saginaw. Pursued by many schools, he decided to stay close to home and chose Alma, a small, academically rigorous liberal arts college. As a quarterback, he broke virtually every school record and was invited to training camp by the Chicago Bears and the New York Titans (soon to be the Jets). Instead, he chose baseball. He was already twenty-one when he signed his first pro contract, late for a ballplayer, especially one from a lesser collegiate sports program. By the time Northrup left college, Dick McAuliffe, who is five days younger than Northrup, had already put in four minor league seasons and was playing in Detroit. Northrup became the senior member of the group of prospects who rose through the system together and became the Boys from Syracuse.

"That's what made 1968 so great for us," he says, "and maybe it's something that outsiders don't understand. But that group all knew each other for ten years. When you accomplish something with your best friends, it makes it that much sweeter. That was the satisfaction, the thing that bonded us so closely.

"And it will never happen again. That's the sad part. It's unusual for one guy to stay with an organization for ten years now. For ten guys to do it is impossible. That makes it so much tougher. Because it can be a lonely life. You're on the road with a lot of time to kill. Yeah, a lot of us drank. Nobody took drugs, but a lot of us drank. You can't get away from that. But that wasn't all there was to it. It was a chance to get off among ourselves and talk out our problems. You felt a guy wasn't going so good or maybe doing some things on the field that were wrong. You got to talk to him over a drink, maybe make a suggestion to help him out. You can do that when you feel at ease with the other guys. You feel that you can say these things to them because you know each other so well. That team really didn't need a leader because we were just all growing old together.

"The problem is that after their careers were over it didn't stop for some of the guys. They didn't have the games to give them a release anymore. Hell, some of them played better because they drank. But we had some people who struggled with alcoholism the rest of their lives. It killed them, eventually. They couldn't adjust. I feel sorry for some of these young players making the big money now because they don't know what's in store for them when it ends. Everyone wants to get married and have kids. If you're married and get in at 3:00 A.M. on the road, your roommate doesn't care. But your wife will. Then you have a problem. Everything is at risk. They'll take away everything you have."

Northrup runs a manufacturer's rep business out of a small office in the suburb of Southfield. There is an assortment of

Tigers tickets on his desk as he tries to allot them to clients. The problem is that the way the team is playing it can be tough finding takers. Northrup himself has been cut off by the Tigers. After several years as an analyst on cable telecasts, he lost his job to former teammate Jim Price.

"I have strong opinions," he says. "I've never been afraid to take on the authorities. The caliber of play in so many of these games is so poor that they're hard to watch. I know that when I played, every team had three or four starting pitchers as good as the top guy on most staffs today. So maybe there were some people who didn't like me saying things like that.

"I've always been able to take care of myself, though. I remember going in once to negotiate a contract with Jim Campbell. He started in, like I knew he would, on how I couldn't hit left-handers and why should he pay me more when I could only be a platoon ballplayer. We were $2,500 apart on the contract, and I told Jim that I'd bet him that amount that I hit lefties better than righties. He jumped on it and yelled out to his outer office for his secretary, Alice Sloan, to check it out. She'd been listening to us talk, and she yelled right back, 'I already have and you're not going to like the answer.' But you didn't get one by Campbell too often. Sure, I felt I should have been paid more. Maybe I could have forced a trade. Guys went to the press and did it back then. But what for? You put down roots. For a $5,000 raise, you'd have to pull them up, and after taxes were paid you were left with something like $2,500. Why make an ass out of yourself for $2,500? Money wasn't the object. Hell, the paperboy cashed my series check for me. A rookie will equal my entire earnings in the majors in two and a half years."

Still, the old ties remain. A photograph of a roaring tiger hangs on the wall behind his desk, along with an aerial shot of Tiger Stadium. He also served a term as president of the Tigers alumni. Beside the desk he has a small stack of the conservative magazine *American Spectator*. He is a big fan of Rush Limbaugh and dislikes welfare vociferously.

But at a recent fantasy camp, in which fans get to play the

game with retired Tigers, he was asked to give a brief eulogy for Hank Aguirre, whose uniform was being retired by the campers and presented to his son. Northrup, the man whom his teammates used to call "Sweet Lips" for his sarcastic take on everything, broke down halfway through and couldn't continue.

Likewise his voice turns suddenly tender when he starts to talk about his adopted son, Camille. Northrup and his wife brought him to America from an orphanage in Poland. They were told that his parents were migrant workers who could not care for him because of his medical problems. He was born with an esophagus detached from his stomach. Every meal was a trial because he was unable to keep food down.

"He's doing a little better all the time," Northrup says. "We had the operation to correct his condition. He still has to regurgitate what he eats from time to time, but it's improving. He's such a cute little guy," he says and pulls a picture from his wallet.

The Fox beams with fatherly pride. It is another hit for the Slammer himself, by far the finest of his collection.

CHAPTER 13

Troubled Times

The Tigers wrapped up their troubled West Coast trip on a high note, winning the final three games in Anaheim. One was a shutout by McLain. Even their old nemesis, George Brunet, the man who had throttled their last hope in 1967, was finally put to rest. He was driven out with a four-run barrage in the first inning of the game he started. The Tigers wound up with a 5–1 record against him for the season.

The riddle of how Mayo was going to find playing time for all of his four outfielders also had solved itself. Horton, Stanley, and Northrup were now his everyday unit, and the team thrived. Between May 28 and the All-Star break on July 7, the Tigers would go 31–12. Their lead would swell from ½ to 9½ games. Even the skeptics began to believe.

The Tigers were winning improbably, continuously, relentlessly. One day, Horton hit a seventh-inning homer off Mel Stottlemyre for Detroit's only run, and Lolich, finally pitching an overpowering game, got the 1–0 win. "Horton is the most improved hitter in the league," said the Yankees starter. "He fouled off the best stuff I threw and then hit the mistake out of the park."

Next day, the Yankees bombed starter Les Cain for four runs in the first, then were shut out by Pat Dobson and Fred Lasher on two singles the rest of the way. Detroit kept chipping away, caught New York in the sixth on homers by Horton and Cash, and won it in the seventh on a single by Freehan. They upended Boston, 5–4, giving McLain his ninth win when the Red Sox imploded. Boston made two errors and let in four unearned runs in the seventh inning. Last year, it had been the Tigers who had blown such games.

Alvin Dark, managing just as hard as he possibly could, tried to halt the express when the Tigers returned home for a contest with Cleveland on June 7. With the game tied 3–3 in the eighth inning, Dark ordered an intentional pass for Horton, who had already homered, with two out and nobody on base. The success of that odd move seemed to encourage Dark to scale even greater heights. Nursing a 4–3 lead in the ninth, he saw reliever Mike Paul get the first two outs with no trouble. That brought Freehan to bat. Dark decided he still wanted to keep Paul in the game but preferred that a right-hander, Stan Williams, pitch to Freehan. So he switched Paul to first base. When Freehan singled, Paul was brought back in to face the left-hand-hitting McAuliffe. Nice strategy, but there was a small problem. Dark had used all the first basemen on his roster. So a flabbergasted Lee Maye, an outfielder who had never played first before in the majors, was flung into the game and stationed there. McAuliffe hit a dribbler right to him . . . and Maye promptly kicked the ball away for an error, indicating that there may have been a reason why previous managers kept Maye in the outfield. Now the Tigers were still alive with Stanley at bat. He lifted a pop fly to short right center. Jose Cardenal came racing into the gap from center, missed a shoestring catch, and wound up booting the ball into the right-field bull pen, as both baserunners scored. The Tigers had won their unlikeliest game of the year.

But this game also introduced an ugly tone to the season. When the Indians scored the go-ahead run in the ninth on a disputed play after which Mayo was thrown out of the game by the plate umpire, a rain of garbage began to fall from the upper deck in right. Beer cans and bottles, a corkscrew, fruit, someone's spectacles. Detroit had a reputation for such barrages. The most famous occurred during the seventh game of the 1934 World Series, when fans in left field bombarded Joe Medwick after he had spiked Detroit third baseman Marv Owen. Judge Landis, who was in attendance, ordered Medwick removed so that the game, which had become a rout for the Cardinals, could conclude. But there had been less publicized incidents over the years. Among them was a near-riot during a Yankees game in 1960 when someone threw the back of a grandstand chair at Roger Maris, and members of the New York bull pen had to flee to the dugout to escape the onslaught.

The upper-deck overhang in right was one of Tiger Stadium's most famous features. It was, in fact, copied by the Texas Rangers when they built their new ballpark in the '90s. It gave fans a great view of the action but also brought them, quite literally, over the head of the right fielder. When displeased, those seated there did not hesitate to let fly.

Two weeks later, the situation got even worse. Big crowds had now become the norm. Even a Wednesday night game against Boston brought more than 30,000 into the stadium. It was a balmy June evening. Many fans arrived with picnic baskets and liquid refreshment, and they were in a festive mood. But that mood started to sour in the seventh when Ken Harrelson hit a three-run homer and put Boston ahead, 5–4. Harrelson trotted out to right field after his blast and was met with boos and curses. By the ninth, with the Tigers out of the game, the garbage followed. Harrelson tried to ignore it and assumed his fielding position. Suddenly he leaped forward violently and an instant later a cherry bomb exploded a few feet behind him. It had hit him in the back just before going off. Then another one exploded above his head. He started to trot off the field, but the umpires tried to convince him to stay. Harrelson refused, finally stationing himself right behind the second baseman. An instant later the game ended.

Most fans booed the instigators. Although club officials indicated that such behavior was increasingly becoming common around the league, it seemed to happen most often in Detroit. Campbell announced that all bags subsequently would be subject to a search by stadium guards and that no beer could be brought into the ballpark from the outside. A few malcontents remained convinced that this all was just a massive conspiracy engineered by the ball club and calculated to force them to buy beer at stadium prices.

In the spring of 1968, however, the entire planet seemed to be thrashing in a spasm of violence that left historians grasping helplessly for comparisons. Less than a week after the Tigers left Los Angeles, Senator Robert F. Kennedy was gunned down in the kitchen of the Ambassador Hotel, just hours after winning California's presidential primary. For the second time in two months, major league baseball was asked to cancel or delay games because of a funeral. Hours before littering the field with garbage on June 7, Detroit fans had stood in silent tribute to the slain national leader. The Tigers switched the following game to night so as not to conflict with the funeral. Although June 9 was declared a national day of mourning, baseball played a full schedule. Besides, it was Bat Day in Detroit. Cancellation was out of the question, and the season's largest crowd so far, a throng of 52,938, filled Tiger Stadium, day of mourning or not.

The country's colleges were in turmoil. Student demonstrators invaded the office of Columbia University's president in April, took hostages, ransacked papers, and paralyzed one of the nation's top educational institutions for two weeks. No sooner had this been resolved than French leftists seized control of the Sorbonne, put up barricades in the streets of Paris, and prepared to battle the city's police. Bombs were thrown in the streets of the Latin Quarter, and hundreds of thousands of militant workers joined the students in a general strike. America was still reeling from the Tet offensive of January, which seemed to prove that the country's Vietnam policy was a failure. Antiwar demonstrations increased, and activists promised massive protests during the summer's Democratic nominating convention in Chicago. President Johnson had already announced that he would not seek reelection, forced from office by rising opposition to the war.

Against this backdrop, the throwing of a few cherry bombs seemed like pretty tame stuff.

Nonetheless, Detroit had become a symbol of the times. As more details of the previous summer's riot became known, the city seemed to draw farther apart. The *Detroit Free Press* investigated every one of the forty-three riot deaths and concluded that most of them had resulted from a lack of restraint and discipline by police and National Guardsmen. Even though it was not publishing, the paper was awarded the Pulitzer Prize for its coverage. Moreover, several young black men, held by Detroit police in the Algiers Motel on Woodward in the early hours of the riot, had apparently been executed.

Entire neighborhoods in the city had changed from predominantly white to all-black in a few months as residents rushed for the sanctuary of the suburbs. Black leaders denounced the police department as "an occupying army." Only at the ballpark was Detroit able to come together on anything resembling common ground.

CHAPTER 14

The Healer

Willie Horton excused himself, jumping up from his chair in response to a call from another part of the house. He was gone for about five minutes. "My grandfather," he explained upon his return. "He has a room downstairs."

Several minutes later another call took him away again. "That was Dominique, my granddaughter," he said.

Five generations of family live under Willie's roof. He couldn't be happier. It's a big roof. Horton lives in a fine old house in one of Detroit's most prestigious neighborhoods, Sherwood Forest. There is plenty of room for everyone.

He sells machinery, and his employer, who is a big baseball fan, prepared a special packet outlining Horton's accomplishments and career. Not that anyone in Detroit really would need it. Horton is a special man in the city, a symbol of the best that Detroit would like itself to be. "I believe that the 1968 Tigers were put here by God to heal this city," he says, and he is utterly sincere. If anyone could have been named the designated healer, it was Horton.

Hardly a player in the history of the Tigers was not booed in Detroit. Kaline heard it, and so did Hank Greenberg. McLain and Lolich knew what it sounded like, and Cash knew only too well. But not Horton. He was the kid who came off the streets, an almost mythic figure, a natural who never fell from grace. Instinctively, reflexively the crowds knew that Willie Horton was one of them. And for all the years he played in Detroit, they loved him for it.

How odd that long after his retirement his name should be confused with that of a vicious killer and rapist, a paroled criminal who became a divisive political and racial issue during the presidential election of 1988.

"That did bother me," says Willie. "I think Johnny Carson or somebody called me up, and we talked about it on the air and I think we got that all cleared up. But you don't like to see that happen to your good name."

He came out of Northwestern High, maybe the toughest of all the city's schools in the early '60s. Most of the 1967 rioters lived in that neighborhood. The principal of an adjacent Detroit school, also noted for its hard characters, once described it this way: "At my place, if a kid wears a nice leather coat to school, they'll break in to his locker to get it. At Northwestern, they'll rip it right off his back." But just a few blocks away from Northwestern were the studios of Motown Records, which was starting up just as Horton was graduating. There were both hope and despair in those streets.

"We've all got a part to play in life as individuals," he says. "If there's anything I've learned, that's it. You've got to find what you love and do it well. I wish maybe it could have worked out that I work with kids a bit more than I do. Children need heroes today. That's the big need. I had a job with the Police Athletic League in Detroit, setting up baseball teams all over the city and getting them equipment. They just don't play ball anymore in the city the way I used to when I was growing up, and that's a shame. They let the grass grow up on all those diamonds, and the backstops are falling down. It hurts me to see that. Baseball can help these kids.

But, you know, a new mayor got elected here, and I lost that job. I knew the new mayor, Dennis Archer, very well. But he told me that it was a political thing and there wasn't anything he could do. I didn't care about myself. It was the kids.

"When I was growing up my hero was Rocky Colavito. I loved to go out there and watch him hit home runs. When I joined the Tigers I went over and shook his hand. He smiled at me and told me that when I came up to stay, he'd be traded. I couldn't believe it. Trade the Rock? No way. But that's just what happened. They traded my hero to make room for me. Sometimes that happens in life.

"It's funny how people are. When I coached with the Yankees, we had to meet almost every day with George Steinbrenner. I know what his reputation is, but he was always very nice to me. I think he's just a lonely man. I think that's why he acts the way he does sometimes, to draw people to him some way."

As it was for so many of the younger Tigers, 1968 was a break-out year for Horton. He would never again equal the thirty-six homers he hit then, and only twice in his career would he stay healthy enough to play in more games. In the Year of the Pitcher, Horton was a most dangerous character. He was fourth in the league in hitting and RBIs, second in homers and total bases. He combined power and average better than anyone else in the American League.

Horton lost his parents in an auto accident on a snow-covered highway just months before his first full season with the Tigers. His dad, Clint, loved baseball and transmitted that love to his son. When Willie joined the Tigers, he wanted to get his father box seats for a game with Baltimore. Clint Horton wouldn't hear of it, insisting that he watch Willie play from his usual seat in the faraway center-field bleachers. He cheered silently until Willie tagged one off Robin Roberts in the late innings for a home run. Then Clint couldn't hold it in anymore. He leaped to his feet yelling: "That's my boy down there. That's my boy, Willie." The spectator beside him was unimpressed. "If that's your boy down there," he asked, "what are you doin' up here?"

The family had little money, but Clint ran a tight house. He was a disciplinarian, knowing what baseball could do for his son. Willie loved boxing as much as baseball as a teenager. He sneaked across the river to Windsor, Ontario, and fought in some amateur bouts under an assumed name. Unfortunately, the fights were picked up on Canadian television, and when Clint tuned in and saw his son with the gloves on, he went through the roof. That ended Willie's pugilistic career, but whenever there was a fight on the field during his years with Detroit, everyone first looked around to see where Willie was and stayed far away from him.

If Detroit loved Willie, he was always a man looking for family to love. For several years after the death of his parents, Charlie Dressen and Jim Campbell were his father figures. "I talked to Jim practically every day for many years," he says. "If you had a problem you could always go to him. He knew about things. He could separate being my friend from being my boss, the person from the executive. I knew he would always treat me fair when we negotiated a contract. But he made sure that [Federal Appeals Court Judge] Damon Keith was looking out for my interests.

"I started holding barbecues at the Holiday Inn during spring training for the team. I guess it became a regular thing. A way to draw us closer together. That bunch in '68, though, we were close-knit. You saw two Tigers, and you saw all of them. Always talking baseball. What do you do in this situation? How do you react on the field? I loved talking about the game with Kaline. I looked at him like Abraham Lincoln. It was an incentive just to come up to his level of expertise.

"I still hear talk about my throw in the World Series, the one that got Lou Brock at the plate in the fifth game. They say that turned the series around. But that just came out of talking about the game, preparing yourself for what could happen. We'd been told that Brock had got himself into bad habits on the bases. Outfielders had just given up trying to make a play on him because he was so fast getting from second to home. So a lot of times he wasn't watching his coach at third, and the on-deck hitter wasn't coming out to give him the sign to slide or stand up. He almost never slid. We saw these things. It didn't happen by accident. When I threw that ball, I knew we had a shot at him. My job was to hit Coyote [Don Wert] right on the nose and for Freehan to make the call on whether to let it go through or not. It was all in the preparation.

"I see players today taking everything so lightly. Making those one-handed catches. What's that? That's an emergency catch. What can you do with the ball after you catch it one-handed? You respect every pitcher you face. Whatever he has he's going to throw his best to you. You've got to anticipate that. I don't believe there's anybody talking to these young players about these things the way we used to do it."

In the months after the riots, Horton came under tremendous pressure from members of the black community to become a racial spokesman. It wasn't in his nature to be a militant. He didn't feel that he should be representing anyone. His advisor, Judge Keith, tried to shield him from a lot of that. But Horton felt a responsibility that he couldn't quite define to play a spokesman's role. He was aware that people looked to him as a symbol, but he didn't know what kind of a symbol, or what he was supposed to do about it beyond playing ball. In 1969, the pressure was so high that he walked off the team for several days to pull his emotions together. But in the years between, he has grown into a man very much at peace with himself, a grandfather eleven times over, the patriarch of a good house.

"Everything I have in life, I got from baseball," he says. "I always felt if I didn't stay focused, didn't get the most mileage out of my ability, that I was cheating on myself. And I've been repaid many times over. You know, little children five and six years old come up to me, and they know about Willie Horton. That's priceless. But I think it's because of what we gave to this community back then. Those were special times."

CHAPTER 15

Reason
to Believe

There are certain cities in which sports enthusiasts learn early in life to distrust happiness. New Yorkers expect to win, and when they don't they demand loudly to know why not. Los Angeles is a place where the sense of anticipation also runs high ... and if things don't work out, hey, it'll be sunny again tomorrow. Detroit knows no such assurance. It is a city that goes through life feeling that just as things seem to be going well, a safe is probably about to fall on you from a great height. As George Will once wrote memorably about another team, "Being a Cubs fan proves that man was not put on this earth for pleasure." Tigers fans also come to understand that suffering profits the soul and that behind every strip of cheery wallpaper there is an awfully big glob of paste.

The last pennant for Detroit had marched home from the war with Hank Greenberg in 1945. But there was a chalky taste to the triumph. The World Series played that October with the

Cubs has been described, perhaps unfairly, as the worst in history. Wartime players still dominated the rosters of both teams. They made errors, they fell down, they pitched poorly. The war was over, and America was eager to return to good times. But the series was a reminder of the deprivations that the country had just come through and wanted to put far behind it as quickly as possible. Both winners and losers were ridiculed.

There was a tradition in Detroit, however, about the only other world champions in the city's history, the 1935 Tigers. Because of its industrial base, Detroit was savaged worse than any other American city by the Great Depression. The great factories ran with skeleton crews. No one had money to buy the cars they made. The city was devastated, inhabited by an army of the unemployed. Into this picture of despair came a baseball team. Its infield was called the Battalion of Death—Greenberg, Charlie Gehringer, Billy Rogell, and Marv Owen. It was powered by the G-Men—Greenberg, Gehringer, and Goose Goslin. It was led by Black Mike Cochrane, a swashbuckling catcher who refused to countenance defeat and drove his team to consecutive pennants. These men taught a defeated city how to hope again. They brought solace to people who had lost almost everything. And they were loved more than any group of athletes in Detroit's long sports history. Over the years they turned into mythic figures, the paradigm of what ballplayers should be. For an entire generation of men and women, there would be no manager like Cochrane, no slugger like Greenberg, no infielder like Gehringer, no pitcher like Schoolboy Rowe. After Cochrane's death in 1962, the street that ran behind the left-field line at Tiger Stadium was renamed in his honor. When Gehringer and Greenberg passed away, the city's newspapers carried front-page eulogies, and aging children wept silently to themselves. Even the champion Lions and Red Wings teams of the 1950s could not rival them in public affection—because they had saved a city.

As the 1968 season wore into summer and the first anniversary of the riots, it seemed as if the same sense of wonder was building around this baseball team. There was no danger of another racial upheaval. The city was too exhausted for that. But tiny segments of shattered community were slowly crystallizing around the Tigers. Their struggles and defiant last-gasp comebacks seemed to reflect the reborn hopes of the city in which they played.

The crowds were back, bigger than anything Detroit had experienced in the past. Unusually good weather—not a single early season rainout, which was almost unheard of—and the team's fast start were finally bringing fans in after the early attendance lull. In 1968, most franchises still measured success by a one million total at the gate. In this era before free agency, a ball club could profit quite handsomely with that attendance. In a few places—Cleveland, Yankee Stadium, Los Angeles— given a big metro area, a big stadium, and a consistent winner, some teams had crashed through the two million mark. But that was highly improbable in the case of Tiger Stadium.

Although baseball had been played on the site since 1896, the ballpark had existed in its current form for only thirty years. A massive redesign by Walter O. Briggs, which closed in the entire stadium and added a grandstand in right field in 1938, turned it into one of the largest in the majors in seating capacity. Only Cleveland and Yankee Stadium had more than its 52,220. The problem was that a lot of the seats were pretty bad. More of them were in fair territory than in any other park. Many more were obstructed by posts that supported the wraparound upper deck. These posts were situated much lower in the stands than in similar parks, several rows closer to the field than in stadiums of similar vintage in Chicago and Boston. Whereas a fan in an upper-deck box at Tiger Stadium had one of the finest views in the major leagues, a fan just a dozen rows behind him might catch the game only in glimpses from around massive poles. Moreover, the ticket department functioned as a semi-independent fiefdom. Choice seats were withheld from general sale so that ticket takers could accept payoffs at the windows. The practice annoyed and antagonized the customers, but it was tolerated by the ball club. For all these reasons, it would take an extraordinary attraction for the Tigers to sell out for any game and an unlikely combination of events to produce a season of two million fans.

On July 19, one such event occurred. Almost 1,000 more fans than the listed capacity jammed into the park. (That was still 5,000 short of the stadium record, however, because a series of remodelings had eliminated several thousand outfield seats.) It was a Friday night game with Baltimore. The Tigers still had a 7-game lead, only 2½ less than their peak. But they had just come off a poor 3–5 western swing. Meanwhile, the Orioles had canned Hank Bauer who had managed them to the 1966 championship. He was replaced by thirty-seven-year-old Earl Weaver, a feisty little veteran of their farm system. The core of the Baltimore team was the same as that of the winners of two years before. Frank and Brooks Robinson, Boog Powell, Jim Palmer, Davey Johnson, Paul Blair. They had enormous talent. But the Orioles were hit by injuries in 1967 and slid out of contention. They had started out the same way this year. But Weaver lit a fire under them. They were closing ground on the Tigers, and it was with a certain sense of unease, a fear of impending disaster that had become part of the local tradition, that the big crowd arrived at the ballpark.

The opener of the critical four-game series matched Lolich against Wally Bunker. But Lolich was still struggling. The left-hander was 7–5, with only a handful of strong outings. This was not to be one of them. Frank Robinson reached him for a two-run homer in the third, and Lolich was pulled from the game in the sixth in the midst of another two-run rally. The Tigers trailed 4–0. Moreover, Bunker had yet to give up a hit. In the sixth, however, he walked Wert, and then McAuliffe found the stands in right. With their first hit of the game, the Tigers were right back in it, 4–2.

But Eddie Watt, the top Baltimore reliever, came in and shut the Tigers down again. The lead held up into the ninth. Then Northrup led off with a single, and Kaline, being used as the regular first baseman in place of the slumping Cash, drew a walk. That brought up Cash, who had been inserted into the game a few innings before. Weaver beckoned for left-hander John O'Donoghue to deal with him, and Cash hit into a force-out. With Freehan the next hitter, Weaver went to his other right-handed closer, Moe Drabowsky, to get the last two outs. A journeyman starter for most of his career, Drabowsky, armed with a new and nasty slider, had turned into a top reliever in 1966. His relief job in the first game of the series that year, in which he struck out eleven Dodgers in a bit more than six innings, helped start the Orioles on their upset sweep of Los Angeles. He was especially tough on right-handers. He retired Freehan on another force-out, which scored Northrup from third and closed the Baltimore lead to 4–3. But there were now two outs, and the next hitter was Tom Matchick.

The Tigers shortstop situation had turned into a three-man carousel with no brass ring. Ray Oyler had stopped hitting completely and by now was pretty much limited to late-inning defensive work. Dick Tracewski played mostly against left-handed pitching. Matchick started fairly regularly against right-handed pitching. But there really was no telling who would turn up there on any given day. Sometimes Mayo matched up against pitchers, and sometimes he seemed to go by phases of the moon. He was desperate to find any kind of punch at the position. Matchick, a rookie, was not as accomplished defensively as the others but was hitting about fifty points higher. Not that this was anything to write home about. He finished the season at only .203. But the other two didn't hit at all. Oyler, in fact, went hitless for the entire months of August and September. He would never get another hit in a Detroit uniform.

Matchick had been stuck at the AAA level for three seasons. But after he made the All-Star team with Toledo in 1967, the Tigers could not bring themselves to send him down again. Moreover, he played the game with zest and enthusiasm. He looked like Huck Finn with a fielder's glove, a red-haired throwback to earlier times. But this Huck was almost twenty-five and running out of time to establish himself in the majors. Even if Mayo had wanted to pinch-hit for him now, the bench was empty. Gates Brown had been used, Cash was already in the game, and Eddie Mathews was on the disabled list. Matchick was it.

Miles across the city, three generations of the Grossman family had gathered at the home of their father, Harry, to celebrate his seventy-second birthday. As in many homes in Detroit that night, they were keeping one ear to the radio. Ice cream and cake had been served, and as Matchick came to bat, Laura Grossman was preparing a tray of soft drinks for her family in the den.

Matchick managed to fight Drabowsky to a full count. The big crowd was screaming, imploring the rookie to keep the inning alive. He lifted the next pitch to right field, and the crowd seemed to sag. It was just a routine fly ball to Frank Robinson. But it kept carrying in the humid air, kept drifting toward the overhang less than 325 feet from home plate. The screams turned to dead silence. Everyone in the park on both sides waited in agonizing suspense to see where the ball would land. Robinson had backed up flush against the wall, below the overhang, as the ball descended toward his glove.

At that moment, Laura Grossman walked into the den with her tray full of drinks. Her family was clustered around a small radio, waiting for Ernie Harwell's call. Finally, after what seemed like an hour, just as Laura entered the room, they heard Harwell cry out: "Home run. Tigers win." The entire Grossman family leaped to their feet, waving their arms and screaming. The startled hostess threw up her hands in alarm and horror, fearing that her family had collectively gone mad. Drinks went flying all over the room, splattering against walls, into sofa pillows. The Grossmans collapsed in soggy laughter, trying to calm their mother, yelling in glee at the sheer delight of the moment.

At Tiger Stadium, no one wanted to go home. The entire crowd was still standing and cheering long after Matchick had circled the bases, was surrounded by his teammates, and pummeled into the dugout. If you ask Tigers fans about their memories of the 1968 season, aside from the World Series, this is the game that most will recall. This is the night, they will tell you, when they truly believed for the first time that this team could not lose.

What is generally forgotten, however, is that Baltimore turned right around and swept the next three games. Matchick's homer, in reality, settled nothing. In exactly one week, the teams were at it again, in Baltimore, and the Orioles had shaved another game and a half off the lead. Now it was Earl Wilson on the spot, starting against Baltimore's hottest pitcher, Jim Hardin.

Detroit jumped off to a 2–0 lead, but Wilson had to pitch his way out of trouble in almost every inning. In the sixth, after a single by Mark Belanger and a walk to Frank Robinson, Mayo decided on a change. He went to his young left-hander, Warden, to face Powell. But another single loaded the bases with nobody out. Once again, the team had arrived at a defining moment, a point at which it seemed that the season was in danger of crumbling away. The man called in to hold it together was Daryl Patterson.

The rookie was partly of Native American ancestry. So the rest of the Tigers called him "Fugawe." That was a reference to a running gag from Johnny Carson about a tribe who got its name from being constantly lost, and who, when asked its identity, would repeat only: "Where the Fugawe?" With his crew cut and gangly look, Patterson had been the perfect foil for the veterans throughout the season. One of the time-honored Tigers traditions, for example, was to tell rookies on the first evening of a warm-weather visit to Chicago to be sure to show up for the team boat ride at 8:00 P.M. The veterans would then gather in a nearby bar and watch the fun, an urban version of a snipe hunt. The rookies would wait in mounting concern and anxiety as the appointed hour came and went with no boat and no other teammates showing up. Some of them held on for more than an hour before it dawned on them that their boat had already sailed. Patterson had been one of these.

But on this muggy night on the Chesapeake, he was handed the helm. He was the lone success of Charlie Dressen's obsession with signing "tough" ex-National Leaguers. Dressen had seen him pitch as a farmhand with the Dodgers and was impressed by his fastball. Even more, he liked him because of his "mean face." The Tigers drafted him on that recommendation, and for once Dressen's instincts were right. Patterson was a tough character and did not hesitate to come inside with his hard stuff. He would end the year with seven saves, tops on the Tigers along with Dobson. This save was the most memorable.

The first man he faced was pinch hitter Fred Valentine, who had just come over in a trade with Washington. After Valentine would be Brooks Robinson and Johnson. Patterson blew them all away. In one of the great displays of power pitching the Tigers had seen all year, he struck out the side, getting each of them on high fastballs. Then he finished out the game by giving up just one hit, and the Tigers coasted home, 4–1. Next day they hit five home runs behind McLain, winning 9–0. Just like that the lead was back in the safety zone, at 7½ games.

Mayo had been worried about relying too much on his young, untested arms in the bull pen. In June, the team had picked up thirty-three-year-old John Wyatt from Boston. Earlier on this same day, they obtained thirty-eight-year-old Don McMahon from the White Sox. He had been a teammate of Mathews on the championship Braves teams of the late '50s and could still throw hard. He would get into twenty games for Detroit in the last two months of the season, and Wyatt would appear in twenty-two. But as Patterson demonstrated graphically, when the game was on the line, Detroit would still depend on the young guns—him, Warden, Lasher, Dobson, and Hiller. They would be the ones to bring the Tigers home.

CHAPTER 16

The Gater

If the game was close, the rumbling would start in about the eighth inning. This was the Tigers' time throughout the 1968 season. This was when they were especially dangerous. In a season when pitchers dominated, Detroit sent up a lineup in which almost every batter could hit a home run. Eight of them were in double figures. No other team in baseball came close to that kind of sustained power. When low-run games were the norm, the Tigers could score in quick bunches. About four of every ten wins came on their last time at bat. One mistake could get them back into a game.

But one man seemed to do it better than anybody else. When he got off his seat in the dugout and moved toward the bat rack, the rumbling in the stands would begin to grow louder. When his stocky form mounted the steps onto the field and headed toward the on-deck circle, it turned to a roar. And when Gates Brown started walking to the plate it built to a frenzy, a release of anticipation that had been growing for two hours. From the second game of the season, when his ninth-inning homer beat Boston, it had started. This was the moment fans had waited for. When the game was on the line, it was Gates's hour.

But as he looks back now, he feels that his hour never really struck.

"That was never my dream," says Brown. "Being a pinch hitter. Sitting on the bench for the whole game and then getting one swing. Who would want that? I wanted to play. Everyone who ever dreams of getting to the major leagues wants to be a star. No one sees themselves spending a career sitting on the bench.

"But they made up their minds, and there wasn't anything I could do to change it. I couldn't play in the field. That was it. Can you remember any time when they put me in the outfield and lost a game because of it?"

His listener says that he can't.

"Thank you," says Gates.

The lunch hour is almost over at Carl's Chop House, a venerable Detroit restaurant that specializes in meat and plenty of it. When he arrived for his appointment, Gates immediately requested a switch to the smoking area of the restaurant. "Can't get through a meal without a smoke," he said. He only picked at his steak and eventually wrapped up half of it to take home. As he spoke about the past, his anger crowded out his appetite.

"I pleaded with them to trade me," he says. "I'd go in to Jim Campbell's office and tell him I heard that Cleveland was interested in me and please, please make a trade. He told me that no one wanted me. I was just the twenty-fifth man on the roster.

"Racism pervaded that organization. They'd tell you jokes with the N-word in them while they were instructing you. You never opened your mouth. When they went to pass out the series tickets, the black fans somehow got shut out. I don't know how they did it. Must have looked at the postmark and tossed the Detroit envelopes out."

This accusation was made at that time because of the small number of black faces in the stands during the series. The Tigers

heatedly denied it. The real explanation is probably less con-
spiratorial than that. Series ticket sales are controlled by such a
small group of individuals and businesses that the average fan
must, inevitably, have some kind of inside connection to get a
seat in any city. Very few black people in Detroit were well connected in corporate or political life in 1968.

"You know," says Gates, "that the only ones with series rings
from both 1968 and 1984 are me and Dick Tracewski. We both
played in one and coached in the other. I'm proud of that. But
after we won in '84, when I was the hitting coach, and money
was flowing all over the place, you know what they offered me
as a raise? Twenty-eight hundred dollars. Players are making
millions, and they were still treating me like their boy. I turned
'em down and walked away from it. Because if I took that kind
of raise they'd have been right. And I ain't nobody's boy.

"They never gave me the credit. When Lou Whitaker and
Alan Trammell came up to the Tigers they were both slap hitters. They didn't know how to turn on the ball. The Tigers were
happy with their five homers a year. But they both became big
hitters. They could drive twenty homers regularly. Now who
was the hitting coach when that was going on?"

You were, says his companion.

"Thank you," says Gates.

Memory is deceiving. Gates pinch-hit just thirty-nine times
during the 1968 season and came to bat a mere ninety-two
times. Pitcher Earl Wilson batted fewer times, drove in more
runs, and hit more homers. Yet Gates is a shining symbol of that
year. When the Standard Club, an organization of Jewish busi-
nessmen, chose someone to honor in 1968 with the presentation of a new car, it picked Gates. He represented, they said, the
highest aspiration of athletics, the man who came through
when it was all on the line. Moreover, his personal triumph—
being scouted and signed by the Tigers out of the Ohio State
Penitentiary after being convicted of a youthful crime—was an
inspiration to the entire city.

The stats tell just part of the story. When he did pinch-hit, he batted .462. Half of his eighteen pinch hits were for extra bases, and three of them were homers. Only once did he strike out. When he delivered, he did it with flair.

The August 11 doubleheader against Boston was Gates's apotheosis, the day that belonged to him alone. Boston had battered Wilson with a four-run first inning in the opener. But slowly, laboriously the Tigers struggled back into it. Wayne Comer drove starter Jim Lonborg out of the game in the seventh with his only home run of the year, and then Don Wert tied it in the eighth with a triple. Meanwhile, five Detroit relievers blanked the Red Sox.

The game went into extra innings, beyond the four-hour mark. After Wert tied it, Detroit could get only one more baserunner. Sparky Lyle and Lee Stange stopped the Tigers cold. Stange got the first two men in the fourteenth with Lolich as the next hitter. Mayo had used six pitchers the day before. The bull pen was exhausted. There was no fresh arm to bring in. It was time for Gates. He had to end it now. He pulled Stange into the upper deck in right. Game over.

After the debilitating opener, Mayo decided to give Gates a rare start in left field for the second game. This one went into the ninth tied 2–2. Then Boston rallied for three against Wyatt and Warden, and the fans started shuffling out. It had been a very long day, and they were satisfied with the split and the drama of the opener. But in the bottom of the ninth it started again. With one out after a leadoff walk, the Tigers ran off five straight singles. The Red Sox changed pitchers four times to try to stop the onslaught. Those fans who were departing stopped where they were to watch the denouement.

Kaline tied it with a single, and then Lyle came in to face Brown. Lyle was one of the top relievers of the era, just the sort of tough left-hander whom Brown wasn't supposed to hit. But he drove the ball through the right side for the winning single. Game two over. Tigers win, 6–5. Both games of the doubleheader end on hits by Brown.

"That was my job," he shrugs. "That's what they paid me for.

I don't give a damn about batting average. Show me how the man hits with a runner on second. That's how you measure. How do you hit when the game is riding on what you do? But I was on a mission that year. I'd missed a lot of '67 with a bad wrist. I knew that one pinch hit could have made the difference, the way that race went. After spring training they tell me that I just made the team. That it had come down to me or Lenny Green. Nothing against Lenny, but I thought they were crazy. I was an angry man. I was going to show 'em once and for all how wrong they were about me. After the season, Campbell doubled my pay. I went from $18,000 a year to $36,000. I played seven more seasons and never got to forty. I was stuck. I guess I wasn't the only one. How do you think it made Cash feel, after all those years with the club, when they sat him down in the stretch in '67? Or poor Ray Oyler. Sit him down for the World Series for an outfielder. How did that make him feel?

"They told me that the designated hitter rule was coming in and that it was made for me. It worked for one year. I was the DH in 1973, hit twelve homers, drove in fifty runs, got the most times at bat since I was breaking in. Then the next year Kaline was going for 3,000 hits, and he couldn't run anymore. So it didn't take any genius to figure out who the DH would be. Good old Gates would sit down again. After that, it was too late. I was thirty-six years old, it was over for me. I never got that chance."

Brown still lives in the same Detroit house ("I'm happy in the ghetto") he bought as a player. He has not worked since leaving the Tigers after the 1984 season. A plastics company he invested in went bankrupt. Still, none of the aura has faded. During the course of lunch, a steady stream of diners stopped by the table. They just wanted to shake Gates's hand, say hello, tell him that they remember.

"It's funny the things that bother me now," he says. "I always prided myself on being ready whenever they called on me. Except that when Billy Martin managed that team there was never any telling what he would do. He'd play Hitler if he could win a ball game for him. He sent me up to hit for Willie [Horton] in the 1972 playoffs, and I never expected it. For Willie? Come on. One of the best clutch hitters in the game? I never saw it coming, and I wasn't focused. I popped up and killed a rally. We lost the playoffs and a chance to get back to the series by one run. That haunts me. I failed.

"In the later years, you know, Campbell used to call me about once a week from Florida. After he was retired. He must have really been bored if he wanted to talk to me. I guess you could call our relationship kind of a love-hate sort of thing. We had our moments. After he died, they told me that he'd left me a little something and that he'd wanted me to be a pallbearer. Only four players showed up for his funeral—me, Freehan, Wilson, and Kaline [who gave a eulogy]. I guess that tells you what they thought of him. If he hadn't asked for me I don't know if I'd have gone."

Somehow, it doesn't square. It seems a shame that a man who once was chosen as a symbol of character should be left with such bitter memories of those times. His luncheon companion tells him that upon parting. He would always remember Brown, he says, as a kind, considerate man who would go out of his way to help someone with a problem.

"Thank you," says Gates.

CHAPTER 17

Deadline USA

The first week of August brought a comeback that was not entirely welcomed by the Tigers. The newspaper strike was over. The two dailies were back in business after a work stoppage of almost nine months. Eager to regain readers and advertisers, both papers pounced on what had become, unquestionably, the biggest local story of the year—the Tigers. Columnists and sidebar writers were attached to the team full time. In the words of one editor, "We are going to cover every game from now on with five men and a small dog." Promotions were developed to piggyback on the excitement. The *Free Press* began a Magic Moment contest in which readers were invited to pick the exact date, hour, and minute at which the Tigers would clinch the pennant. First prize was two tickets for the series. The paper also revived a popular feature from the sports pages of the '30s—Iffy the Dopester. This persona, developed by a former managing editor, the late Malcolm Bingay, had enchanted readers of another era. Writing in a style best described as part Damon Runyon and part Bugs Bunny, Iffy had become a literary symbol of those earlier Tiger triumphs. Now he was resurrected as a link to the treasured past for both the paper and the city.

The Detroit clubhouse, however, was not altogether idyllic. Cash was still grumpy about his shortage of playing time. McLain's star turns were beginning to get on everyone's nerves. Lolich was still struggling and in August was exiled to the bull pen—just as he was at about the same point of the 1967 season. For those who looked down the road, a more serious disruption loomed with the recovery of Kaline. Mayo was once more called upon to juggle four healthy starters for three outfield positions.

But the unhappiest man in the Detroit clubhouse was Joe Sparma. The pitcher had a penchant for driving his managers crazy. He threw harder than any other Tiger starter, and when he was good he was very, very good. But when he was bad, he was all over the place. He could not locate home plate with a compass and a metal detector. After one such performance a few years before, interim manager Bob Swift had raged, "The son of a bitch looks like he never threw a baseball before in his life." Sparma played winter ball before the 1967 season and came to spring training in a groove. He went 16–9, his best year by far, and pitched five shutouts. But in 1968 it was the old Sparma who showed up once more. In one start he would be overpowering and, in the next, struggle to get past the third inning. An exasperated Mayo finally took him out of the rotation. "I can't start him, and he's too wild to pitch relief," he complained. "What am I supposed to do—take him out and shoot him?"

"You couldn't even play catch with the guy," says John Hiller. "He'd have to come to a pitching set just to throw the ball back close enough for you to catch. Same thing when he threw to first on a ball hit back to him. When he played for Montreal, Gene Mauch wanted to station his shortstop in back of the catcher when Joe gave an intentional pass. He never knew where the ball was going to wind up. It was all mental with him. When he was on, he had better stuff than Nolan Ryan. He just never figured out how to harness it."

What especially infuriated managers was a perceived lack of seriousness on Sparma's part. There was also a suspicion that he could stand to lose a few pounds and that part of his problem was that he was out of shape. He was the cheeriest of men, something of a gourmand when the bill of fare featured pasta. He was also among the Tigers not known to turn away a drink. He didn't shave before his starting assignments, and with a thick growth of black beard, he did his best to glower from the mound. But it all was an act. He was, in reality, a pussycat.

He had been a high school star in Massillon, a quarterback who went on to play for Woody Hayes at Ohio State. But Sparma's strong point was the passing game. Hayes, of course, regarded the pass as a confession of weakness, used only by lesser schools that did not recruit offensive linemen. He played Sparma infrequently. So Sparma left school as a junior to sign a baseball contract. Although his minor league record was only 4–9, it took him just a season and a half to reach Detroit. Anyone who threw that hard just had to win.

But all the promise seemed like a memory now. Sparma felt that he was being picked on; alone of all the starters, he was the one in whom Mayo had no confidence. Worse yet, the manager gave him no clues. He complained privately about the lack of communication with his manager to his close friend, Freehan, and brooded about it endlessly. The blowup came on August 14. Sparma had been knocked out early in two previous starts but also had pitched rather effectively in a long relief assignment, striking out five Red Sox in less than three innings. So he was given another chance to start in Cleveland against Luis Tiant, who already had shut out the Tigers twice. Mayo did not want Tiant to get a lead. Freehan put Detroit into an early 1–0 advantage with a homer. But it was a typical struggle for Sparma. Through three innings, he struck out three and walked two. He got another strikeout to start the fourth. Then Jose Azcue singled, and suddenly Lolich was up and throwing in the bull pen. Sparma watched him, puzzled, and seemed to lose his concentration. When Max Alvis followed with a walk, Mayo made his way to the mound. He called for the ball from a disbelieving Sparma and brought in Lolich.

Sparma was furious as he sat in the clubhouse. He had nowhere to go because the team would fly to Boston right after the game. He had a beer, and then a few more. When the game ended with a 3–0 win, Lolich giving up just three singles the rest of the way, Sparma was still steamed. He felt he had been humiliated, that his manager had failed to tell him what was expected of him. On the flight east, he sat down next to *Free Press* columnist Joe Falls and unburdened his soul. Everything that had been bothering him came spilling out. "I don't know if I can play for that man anymore," he said. Falls wrote it as Sparma said it, and the column was played strongly in the following morning's paper.

Reader reaction was unlike anything that a column by the popular Falls had ever received. *The Free Press* was accused of trying to blow the pennant, of wrecking the team's harmony. Caller after caller demanded to know how the paper dared to come back after all these months and ruin things for the Tigers. Many of them cancelled their subscriptions.

Falls was totally oblivious to any of this. He had filed his story, and because there was no game the next day, he and the paper's baseball writer rented a car and spent the afternoon touring the North Shore. Only when he got back to the hotel for his phone messages did he realize what a storm had been stirred up. He was also told that there would be no repeat. Under the direct order of the managing editor, there were to be no more negative stories written about the Tigers this season. Falls was furious, but he was told that the position of the paper in the community was regarded as so tenuous that it simply could not afford to offend its readers with negative news (or, if you choose, honest reporting).

Instead, the paper concentrated on Iffy and the Magic Moment. The following night McLain won his twenty-fifth game of the season and his sixth shutout. He was 15–1 over the last two months and had given up just six runs in his last five starts, all of them complete games.

At times, he seemed almost bored by how easily it was going.

When Boston put runners on third and second in this game, he simply reared back and struck out Dalton Jones, Carl Yastrzemski, and Ken Harrelson. It wasn't even a contest. They couldn't have hit him with a squash racket.

The Tigers had hit a wall after the All-Star Game, going just 5–9 for the next two weeks and allowing Baltimore to sneak back into the race. But now they were on a 17–6 tear and very much in control once more.

The previous weekend, when the Tigers had come back twice to upend Boston in a doubleheader, Gates Brown was standing on first after getting a hit. Red Sox first baseman George Scott sidled up to him and said: "You guys ain't got a thing to worry about. You're gonna win this easy."

But there were still those who worried that asking for the selection of a Magic Moment was a dangerous act of hubris—one that a team that had not won a pennant in twenty-three years may yet come to regret. Fate was being tempted. On the night of August 22, fate selected a most unlikely agent with which to strike back.

CHAPTER 18

Mad Dog

Pulitzer Prize-winning sports columnist Jim Murray once wrote that he had a soft spot in his heart for Dick McAuliffe. Not only did they both come from Connecticut, but the Tigers second baseman also reminded Murray of a bare-knuckled prizefighter. With his old-fashioned open stance and the way he lifted his right foot as the pitch came in and his dark Irish looks, McAuliffe made Murray think of John L. Sullivan.

To Detroiters, a comparison was more readily made with another black-haired Irishman out of New England, Mickey Cochrane. Not only were the ethnicity and geography right, but both also had the same blazing will to win. You saw it in their eyes the moment they stepped across the white lines. If you wanted to beat them you were going to have to come at them and take it away. There would be no gifts.

The Tigers called McAuliffe "Mad Dog," but off the field it was a wildly inappropriate nickname. The personality transformation was amazing. He was a quiet, almost unassuming man. He roomed with Don Wert, another taciturn individual. For them, an exchange of "Good morning" constituted a major conversation. On the field, however, McAuliffe was driven.

"Everytime I go out there," he said, "I tell myself that maybe I'm going to do something today that nobody's ever done before. So I've got to play it to the hilt."

When asked, McAuliffe would talk politely about almost anything. The notable exceptions were injuries, which he would never admit to, and the difficulty he had in picking up the ball when certain left-handers were pitching. In this regard, he was much like Freehan. The catcher had been advised to move in tight on the plate. As a result, he annually led the team in being hit by pitches. It was the one thing that Freehan would not discuss. He didn't want it on his mind, didn't want a simple mention of it to be construed as fear by the opposition. So it was with McAuliffe. Certain lefties gave him trouble, but he refused to accept it, would not discuss it. One of those lefties was Chicago's Tommy John.

"I don't know how many times I've thought about that night," he says in his Florida home. "I always was able to keep it under control on the field. I was never the guy in the middle of the brawl. But there was no doubt in my mind that John was throwing at me and he was doing it under orders. Something just snapped."

It was a getaway night game at Tiger Stadium, a game with Chicago on August 22. The Tigers had handled the White Sox rather easily all year. Hiller had one-hit them a couple of nights before, and Price beat them with a tenth-inning homer the previous evening. McAuliffe was battling a 2-for-18 slump and was given a day off when another left-hander, Gary Peters, had started in the series.

But he led off the first with a single off John and came around to score on two more hits. He batted again in the third with one out and the score still 1–0.

"The first pitch was right at my head," says McAuliffe. "I didn't think anything of it. Probably was a pitch that slipped. Then the second one came up there, too. I was dug in pretty good. I never dreamed that he'd be throwing at me. I remember turning around to the plate umpire, Al Salerno, and saying, 'Jeez, if that one had hit me it would've killed me.'

"We worked the count to 3–2, and here comes another one, right at my head. I went down, and the ball went all the way to the backstop. OK. There's an easy walk, I told myself, and I started trotting to first base. I really don't remember being all that upset about it. I thought it was kind of stupid. But I looked out at John, and he looked back and said: 'What the hell are you looking at?'

"That did it. Next thing I knew I was running out there. I can't really tell you what happened. I guess he must have ducked when he saw me coming, and I hit him on the left shoulder with my knee. I heard him give a cry of pain, and then everybody else was all over us. When it was over, John was walking off the field, clutching his shoulder. I got tossed out of the game, which I knew would happen, and I didn't think anything more about it. It just seemed like one of those things that can happen in a pennant race on a hot night."

But the White Sox were infuriated. It soon became apparent that John, their top starter at 10–5, was lost for the season. There was some speculation that there might be permanent damage, jeopardizing his career.

Chicago General Manager Ed Short immediately filed a complaint with the league office, demanding a suspension of McAuliffe. When McAuliffe checked his mailbox in the hotel in New York the following morning, he found a note from American League President Joe Cronin. It informed him that he was being fined $250 for the incident. That seemed fair enough to the Tigers.

But Short, upon hearing of the fine, hit the ceiling. He phoned Cronin, detailed the injury to John, and demanded a more substantive punishment. A few hours later, the Tigers were notified that McAuliffe would be fined an additional $250 and suspended for five days. That would put him out of the entire four-game

series scheduled in New York and two more against Chicago—
the last two games that the teams would play this season.

Now it was Campbell's turn to rage. He called Cronin at his
office in Boston and informed his longtime friend that he was
"nothing but a fat-bellied son of a bitch." But the suspension
stuck. (John was out for the rest of the year but made a full recovery. Oddly enough, he did blow out his arm six years later, and
again it was thought that his career might be over. Instead, he
became the first player to go through experimental reconstruc-
tive arm surgery and went on to pitch in three World Series.)

Campbell's anger over the suspension was well placed. With all
the power in the Detroit lineup, it was still McAuliffe who made
the engine run. That weekend turned out to be the longest of the
year for the Tigers, one in which the magic ride came dangerous-
ly close to turning back into a pumpkin.

Although McAuliffe was just twenty-eight, only Kaline and
Cash had been with the Tigers longer. An ideal leadoff man, he
knew how to draw walks and was a clever baserunner. He would
lead this team in runs scored with ninety-five. Quick rather than
fast, he also stole eight bases, enough to set the Tigers' rather
leaden pace.

He had played all over the infield after coming to Detroit in
1961 until settling at shortstop two years later. It was a position
chosen for him out of necessity. There were no shortstops in the
system, and although he played it with more enthusiasm than
skill, he was all there was. He got a good jump on the ball, and
his glove was fairly sure. But he did not have an exceptionally
strong arm and, as a result, felt compelled to hurry many of his
plays. He led the league in errors one year and never gave an
indication that he could make the difficult play consistently. But
when Jerry Lumpe retired after the 1966 season, second base was
open. Mayo moved McAuliffe into the vacancy, and it may have
been the most adept switch of his career. McAuliffe blossomed
into an outstanding fielder.

"I was never the most talented guy around," he says. "I wasn't
even the best player on my neighborhood team. But I worked

harder than anybody else. I had some talent, but my strength was that I played the game aggressively. That's the way we did it in Connecticut.

"Even the batting stance came about because I was working at it all the time. My first year in the minors I was hitting everything to left. So Wayne Blackburn, the hitting coach, got hold of me and told me to open up and get my hips out of the way. I started hitting to all fields then. The high step just felt comfortable. People said it reminded them of Mel Ott. Well, he did pretty well batting that way. I think it made my bat quicker.

"If you ask me why we won it in '68, I'd have to say no mental mistakes. We never beat ourselves. Every one of us was into every game, and if we thought someone's head wasn't in the game, he'd be talked to by the rest of us. All winter long I had thought about that double play that ended the 1967 season. It was only the second time I'd hit into one of those all year. I hated double plays. No excuse for a left-handed hitter to do it with the added jump they get towards first. I didn't hit into a single DP in '68. I always liked that stat."

McAuliffe now lives full time in Naples, Florida, after selling his coin washing machine business in Connecticut. He is still trim, still dark-haired while coping with diabetes. But the fire in his eyes burns only on the golf course now. He taught himself to swing cross-handed on the theory that left-handed golfers are at too much of a disadvantage. He is probably the best at the game of any of the former Tigers.

But the fire is far from banked. He appeared at a fantasy camp featuring the '68 team a few years ago. The camp concludes with a game between the big leaguers and the campers, with the old ballplayers always winning in a rout. By the late innings they are usually making outs deliberately, trying to speed things along. Not McAuliffe. A participant in the game said that McAuliffe wound up going nineteen for twenty, refusing to give up an out or an inch. After all, they were playing baseball. That was Mad Dog's game.

CHAPTER 19

The Lost Weekend

Songs have been written about the fresh promise of autumn in New York. But no one will ever write anything good about August in New York. The heat seems to rise from the sidewalk. Not a current of air stirs in the midtown canyons. Apartment dwellers climb to the rooftops to find relief. August was also, traditionally, the time when the hopes of countless baseball teams went to die in Yankee Stadium.

By 1968 the Yankees were no longer the Yankees. They had last won a pennant four seasons before and in 1966 had tumbled, shockingly, all the way to last place. They climbed one rung out of the cellar the following year and seemed to be retooling. At least they were respectable again and playing over .500. A few of the old titans remained. Most notably, there was Mickey Mantle, slowed so much that he was exclusively a first baseman. The series hero of six long autumns ago, Tom Tresh, was at short, and Joe Pepitone had traded positions with Mantle and roamed center field. Mel Stottlemyre remained as a starter from the glory days and so did reliever Steve Hamilton. Otherwise, there were only memories to sustain the Yankees.

But the past has its power, and the stadium could still be an intimidating place. Kaline and Cash had stark recollections of coming there in the summer of 1961, after running with the Yankees all season long and losing three in a row to fall abruptly from the race. The Yankees merely toyed with other contenders in those years, leading them to believe that there was some hope of overtaking them. Then they would get them into the stadium sometime in late summer and off-handedly beat their brains out.

On the Tigers schedule, this late August weekend in New York didn't appear to be an ordeal. A night game on Friday followed by two day games, and then the Tigers were out of there. But a June game had been rained out and rescheduled as part of a twi-night doubleheader on Friday. So when the bus pulled away from the Roosevelt Hotel and began the traffic-clogged passage up Madison Avenue to the Bronx, the Tigers realized there was a long weekend ahead of them. They didn't know the half of it.

This was an unusual weekend in many regards. *Life* magazine was doing a full-scale profile on McLain, and its reporter followed him around full time. His run for thirty wins now stood at twenty-five. It had become the biggest story of the baseball season. The magnitude of his attempt was becoming clear. Only three pitchers in the live ball era—Jim Bagby in 1920, Lefty Grove in 1931, and Dizzy Dean in 1934—had reached that number of wins. The most recent had been thirty-four years ago. Ted Williams had batted over .400 since then, to cite a comparable achievement. Thirty wins was an incredible accomplishment. The story may not have been quite at the level of Roger Maris's run at the Babe's sixty homers in 1961, because it lacked daily drama and the ghost of the game's greatest player to drive it. But it was still big.

In 1968, sports coverage was only a shadow of what it would become in the decade ahead. Television technology did not yet permit the sort of ubiquitous presence that would be common by the end of the '70s. Moreover, baseball was still regarded as a game, not as a marketing strategy. Still, McLain's locker was surrounded by reporters at every stop in the league. He was an ingratiating interview, a young man full of fascinating eccentricities as well as talent. Organist, pilot, and pitcher. He was even a terrific bowler. Denny may have been "Dolphin" to the Tigers, but to the national media he was as big as a whale. On this visit to the media center of the world, his first since becoming a major celebrity, the carnival was fully aglow.

The newly returned Detroit newspapers added to the fun. Trying to coax all it could out of the Tigers story, the *Free Press* assigned a feature writer to accompany the team into New York. That was not unusual. Newspapers did that all the time to give the "human" touch to a big sports story. But the paper was looking for a different angle. The writer assigned this time was a woman.

Mary Ann Weston was a talented young reporter and also quite attractive—willowy, dark haired, and recently married. In 1968, the idea of a woman writing sports and going on the road with a big league team was groundbreaking. Journalism was still twenty years away from assigning women beat reporters to major teams. Women now have full access to locker rooms, in most cases, and their presence is treated as a matter of course. That was decidedly not the case then.

"I always save one hour every semester to discuss the experience with my classes," says Weston, who is now a journalism professor at Northwestern University. "They look at me as if I'm part of living history, which is kind of funny. I couldn't go into the clubhouse then, of course. But they also barred me from the press box and the dugout and the field. They told me each time that 'it was no place for a woman' and that my presence might 'inhibit' some of the players. The whole trip went that way, and it was something that you don't forget."

The Tigers didn't seem to know how to react to the dawn of the feminist age in their world. Weston was permitted to travel on the chartered flight from Detroit to New York and on the team bus. Airplane trips were always rather rowdy affairs after a night game. The players let off steam, and there was usually beer aboard the plane. Ribaldry was the norm, to phrase it politely.

But the players outdid themselves on this trip. Every bawdy ballad and double entendre, every sly sexual innuendo and euphemism that had been laughed at during the season was dusted off and trotted out again for Weston's hearing on this trip. Like schoolboys in the presence of the homecoming queen, the Tigers chortled, guffawed, and poked each other in the ribs. Weston took it all in and pretended not to hear. Her first report was headlined: "Our Tigers Are Charmers." The Detroit newspapers were still determined not to rock the boat with readers' perceptions of their heroes.

Weston says that McAuliffe and Pat Dobson separately took her aside to explain and apologize for some rude remarks she might have heard. Gates Brown asked her to lunch at the Cattleman, a players' hangout a few blocks from the hotel, to make amends. "I felt bad for her the same way I would when anybody is being given a hard time," says Brown. As pioneering experiences go, it was not quite a landmark. But it wasn't a day at the beach, either.

The situation on the field was also deteriorating daily. McAuliffe's suspension was announced by the league office on Friday afternoon. Mayo, already playing with a black hole in his batting order at shortstop, now was faced with the prospect of shifting one of those nonhitters to second base to replace McAuliffe. Moreover, Mayo now had no leadoff man. Stanley, who usually batted second, was elevated to the leadoff spot, and Tracewski was placed at second and hit second. The two of them went 0-for-8 in the first game Friday, and the Tigers lost 2–1 to Stan Bahnsen, their only run coming on a homer by the losing pitcher, Wilson.

In the nightcap, remembering his experiment in spring training, Mayo tried to juice up the attack. He played Stanley at shortstop and got all his big-hitting outfielders into the starting lineup, too. That didn't work much better. The Yanks tied the game at 3–3 on a two-run homer by Roy White in the eighth. Then the offense died on both sides in the oppressive evening heat. Between the eighth and sixteenth innings, twenty-two

Tigers in a row went down, with veteran Lindy McDaniel pitching seven perfect innings. Then Dooley Womack came in and threw four more shutout innings. It was quite likely that the game could have continued until dawn without the Tigers being able to score. But the Yankees could do no better against Hiller and McMahon, who combined on a twelve-inning shutout.

Mercifully, the 1:00 A.M. curfew arrived in the middle of the nineteenth inning. The muggy stalemate was finally halted after the Yanks went out in that inning, and it was ruled a suspended game. It would have to be replayed, to the horror of everyone, as part of a newly scheduled doubleheader on Sunday.

After a very brief night, the teams were back at it Saturday afternoon, with McLain looking for number twenty-six. Instead, he lost, 2–1. It was the first time all year that he had dropped two games in a row. Aside from a two-run, first-inning homer by White, who had become an enormous pest, Denny was never in trouble. But the best that Detroit could do was a solo shot by Horton. Again the team seemed listless without McAuliffe keying the attack from his leadoff spot. It had now scored five runs in thirty-seven innings in New York.

McLain left the stadium in a foul mood, with his tail from *Life* magazine right with him. The two of them headed back to Manhattan in the writer's convertible. At a stoplight they pulled up beside a car with a pretty young woman seated inside. "Hey, honey," barked Denny. "How'd you like to fuck a five-game loser?" The quote, in laundered form, appeared in *Life* the following week, adding to the McLain mystique.

Sunday was the hottest day yet, temperatures over ninety degrees with humidity to match. Instead of playing one and jumping on the jet to Milwaukee, the Tigers knew they had to labor twice. At this point, it seemed that just getting the whole nightmarish weekend over with would be a victory in itself. But the worst was still to come.

The Tigers ripped starter Steve Barber for a quick 5–0 lead in the opener. With his staff still in shreds from Friday's marathon and another game coming right up, Yankee manager Ralph Houk made a desperation move. He brought in Rocky Colavito as a mop-up pitcher.

The Rock was in his last season in the majors. No longer the feared slugger who averaged 121 RBIs between 1958 and 1965, he was just playing out the string. Four of those earlier productive years had been with Detroit. Colavito, teaming with Kaline and Cash, nearly had slugged the Tigers to a pennant in 1961. But after the adulation he had received in Cleveland, he never was quite at home in Detroit. He seemed to resent the reverence in which Kaline was held and the stark fact that he would never be paid as much as the longtime Tigers star. "Who is Kaline, a little tin god?" he had asked angrily during one contract dispute. Colavito had told the young Horton that when Willie was ready for the big leagues Colavito would be traded. He was absolutely right. But now, five seasons later, in a totally unexpected manner, it was payback time.

Colavito had one of the strongest arms in the game. He had pitched once with the Indians in 1958 and threw three shutout innings. He was always fooling around during warm-ups— throwing from a windup, breaking off curveballs. Now he'd have his chance.

He came in with two men on in the fourth, retired his old nemesis, Kaline, and his former admirer, Horton. In the fifth, he walked two, but he kept the Tigers scoreless. In the sixth, Kaline reached him for a double, but Colavito retired Detroit again, striking out Tracewski. Then, in the sixth, the Yankees erupted. They scored five times off Dobson and Patterson and found themselves in front, 6–5. Womack and McDaniel finished up with three shutout innings and—who could believe it—Colavito was the winning pitcher.

"I feel so funky," laughed the Rock in a specially arranged between-game interview. The Tigers felt much worse than that. To a man, when asked to recall this season, they named the defeat by Colavito as its absolute low point. The loss in the second game, in which Colavito played right field and hit a homer and Horton lost a ball in the treacherous left-field glare for a two-run single, was just the final coat of misery. The Tigers had lost again, 5–4—their fourth consecutive one-run defeat of the weekend. Yankee Stadium even in its decline seemed to have snared one more late summer victim. Baltimore again was only five games back. The Tigers were hanging at the edge of the abyss.

When the clubhouse doors were finally opened after the second game, a message had been scrawled on a chalkboard: "If you think the world ended today, you don't belong here."

It was assumed that Freehan, the emotional former football player, had written the words. But Freehan says that the author was Eddie Mathews. The veteran had injured his back in June and not played since. The injury would force his retirement at the end of the season. But while he was on the disabled list he dressed for every game, at home and on the road. He was held in such high regard that every Detroit opponent approved the arrangement, a necessity for road games. Mathews, eventually, would be ruled eligible for the World Series by the commissioner's office. It was a gesture based on sentiment more than anything else for a man who would be voted into the Hall of Fame ten years after this season. He was the first member of this team to go into Cooperstown, although Kaline would follow him two years later. During this perigee of the season, he became Detroit's inspirational leader.

Moreover, McAuliffe's suspension was still not over. It had been extended to cover the Tigers' next two games with Chicago so that there would be no risk of retaliation by the White Sox. The Tigers fumed that the league was trying to pump up interest in a dormant pennant race at their expense. The Tigers bused across the river to Newark and boarded their plane, flying off into the night to a future that suddenly was a lot grimmer than it had been just three days before.

CHAPTER 20

Ratso

A dangerous cigarette dangles from his fingers as he sits at the kitchen table. He knows he shouldn't be smoking. Not with his medical history.

"Ahhh, I gave it up once for about five years," says John Hiller. "Then I got a chance to start a game, and I invited a whole bunch of friends to make the bus trip down from Duluth. They scored five runs off me in the first inning, and I was gone. It was humiliating. I was sitting there in the clubhouse, and someone had a pack in the locker next to me. So I grabbed it, and then I had another one, and then I sent the clubhouse boy out to buy me a fresh pack. I've quit a few times since, but never for that long."

Hiller lives in Iron Mountain, Michigan. The town is five hundred miles from Detroit in the state's Upper Peninsula. But the golf course is just down the street, and the air is fresh. The northern winters may be long, which makes it hard on his leg with the arterial blockage. Still, it is home, and he is happy to be there. A man whom Billy Martin once described as "coming back from the dead," he's happy to be anywhere. A heart attack victim at the age of twenty-seven, informed that his career was over at twenty-eight, no, the cigarette is a mark of defiant life.

"I never liked cities much," he said. "I know a lot of the guys became manufacturer's reps, things like that. But I was never one for schmoozing. I never could bring the same kind of drive that I gave to baseball into business. I tried selling insurance for a while. I just couldn't make it go, even though the name got me in a lot of doors. We had a little farm a few miles outside of town. Raised some stock there. But the leg got so bad, y' know, I just couldn't work it. So I'm just content to let the world go by."

Back in '68 he was Ratso. That was the nickname hung on him by his roomie, Pat Dobson; it was an affectionately sleazy comparison to the Dustin Hoffman character in the film *Midnight Cowboy*. Dobson, in turn, was named Cobra because his pitching motion resembled a snake regarding its prey and then striking. The Tigers were very big on nicknames, some of them bizarre. Jim Price was the Big Guy, reflecting his position as leader of the scrubs. Jim Northrup was not only the Fox but Sweet Lips because of his ongoing acidic commentaries on the world. Horton was 'Roids because of a recurring affliction in his nether regions.

"When Ed Mathews joined the team, they told me to come up with the right nickname for him," says Hiller. "You know, we had a lot of respect for Eddie; but we weren't in awe of him or anything. We knew he was a Hall of Famer and what he had done. But I said, what the hell, let's call him New Guy. So that's what he was. Eddie was with us about a week in 1967, and he said: 'Jeez, you guys aren't going to win any pennant; you're just a bunch of drunks.' That was something coming from him because Eddie never turned down a drink too often. But you know what? Next year he got up and told us, 'I've played baseball for twenty years, and I finally made it to the big leagues.' Isn't that something? From Eddie Mathews. He saw how hard we played the game, y' see. We had our fun, but we knew how to play ball."

Hiller was the last of the '68 winners to stay with the Tigers, the only one who bridged the gap from Mayo Smith to Sparky Anderson. In time, he became the top relief pitcher in the league, one of the first to be used exclusively as a stopper. But then he was in his second year with the team: A self-described "wild man," a kid out of Canada, drinking more than was good for him, running a little amok on the road, and throwing the hell out of the baseball.

"I started, I threw long relief, I pitched short relief," he says. "Whatever they needed. That's how it was. You didn't have the specialists like you do now. A young guy like me got his innings wherever he could. When Mayo decided he couldn't keep Sparma in the rotation for the last two months, I was the number four starter. I pitched a one-hitter, the low-hit game of the year for us. I had the game with Cleveland where I struck out the first six guys and set a record. I made a contribution. That's what made what happened later so tough to accept."

On January 11, 1971, while relaxing at home, he took a deep drag on a cigarette and felt a sharp pain in his chest. An hour later, he lit up again. This time the pain went all around his back. He called his doctor, who said he didn't like the sound of that and told Hiller to meet him at the hospital. So Hiller went outside, unloaded his snowmobile from the car, and drove himself to the hospital.

"When I got there they told me I'd already had three heart attacks," he says. "Of course, I couldn't believe it. I was in my twenties, an athlete. My first thought was that spring training started in about a month, and if the Tigers found out about it they'd be pretty upset. I mean I had no idea what this meant. So I asked everybody to keep it quiet because I thought I'd be ready to go to Lakeland on February 14. Then they told me I had to have surgery. No money in the bank. A family to support. All I knew was baseball. I remember laying in that hospital bed and watching the movie *Brian's Song* on television and crying because I figured that was going to be me. They were just starting this new surgery, an intestinal bypass, which had a chance to clear the arteries without touching the heart. So I said, sure, yeah, anything. Then I had to call Jim Campbell and tell him. It was the day before I was supposed to report.

'Hello, Jim, I guess I won't be coming down.'

'Why not?'

'Because I just had a heart attack.'

'Yeah, sure, you asshole.'

'No, Jim, I really did.'

"Oh, man was he pissed. I don't blame him. But I had the surgery and lost about forty-five pounds. I got a job in a department store to have a little money coming in, but the owners were wonderful and let me work out at the Y, getting my strength back up, as much as I wanted.

"It gave me a chance to think. I hadn't taken care of myself. I was way overweight. Drinking and smoking. I made excuses. Back in '68 we always used to joke that you could take a team picture in the hotel bar. You had a bad game, and you had to take a drink to get over the disappointment. And if you had a good game you sure as hell had to have some drinks to celebrate. You had all that time on your hands on the road. I never drank at home. Oh, maybe a gin and tonic when I got home after a game. But not like on the road, where one drink got to be two and then ten.

"But it was more than that. I always pitched scared. Hell, we all did if you weren't in the starting rotation. You'd pitch over injuries because you didn't want them to know. You'd start thinking that if you had three or four bad games in a row, they'd send you down. You can't pitch that way. But after my heart attack I figured: What can they do to me that would be worse than what I went through? What's there to be afraid of? When a doctor said to me that he doubted I could handle the stress of pitching in the majors again, I told him that wasn't stress. That's what I did for a living, throw a baseball. Whatever happened on the field really didn't mean shit.

"There was this track at the Y in Duluth. Thirty-five laps around was a mile. The first time I tried to run after the surgery

I got around twice and fell flat on my face. I always hated running anyhow. But I just went out there and kept looking at the heels of the guy in front of me and pictured myself pitching again, and I forced myself to run."

After a year, Hiller called Campbell and told him he was ready to go again. Campbell was aghast. Chuck Hughes of the Detroit Lions had died of heart failure on the field during a game at Tiger Stadium the previous fall. Campbell was not eager for a repeat of that. Medical opinion was mixed. People just did not come back from heart attacks and compete at the highest level of athletics. Hiller went through spring training of 1972 as a minor league pitching coach and batting practice pitcher. At the end of training, Campbell reluctantly offered him a job. Pitching coach for the Class A Lakeland farm club. Salary: $7,500 a year.

"I'd been making twenty grand before I got sick," says Hiller. "We bought a house based on that salary. In fact, the series check was my down payment. I told Jim I just couldn't make it on $7,500. He said that's all he could give me, take it or leave it. But I knew I could make it back to the majors. So I took it.

"Here's what I did. I sent my entire paycheck home to Duluth. I got myself a mattress and put it on the floor of the clubhouse in Lakeland. And that was home. After the first night I got a night-light and kept it on all night, because if it was completely dark the roaches would come out. I went to the Tigertown commissary before they broke camp. The cook was a friend of mine. He gave me a big slab of cheese and a big slab of ham and some bread. And that's what I lived on. Ham and cheese sandwiches. It wasn't so bad when we went on the road because then I got five dollars a day meal money. I'd save as much as I could, and when we got back to Lakeland my big treat was to take seventy-five cents, go over to the nightclub, buy one draft beer, nurse it all night, and watch the show.

"A few times I thought to myself: Wait a minute. I pitched in a World Series. I started for a championship team. This is crazy. What am I doing here living like some bum? But Dr. [Clarence] Livingood, the Tigers team physician, was always in my corner.

He used his pull to get me an appointment with this nationally known heart specialist in Atlanta. He was Lyndon Johnson's own doctor. So two days before my appointment, Johnson has a heart attack, and all his appointments are cancelled. That's when I thought maybe it's not meant to be.

"I guess I wasn't much of a coach while this was happening. I was too concerned about my own career. One day I look up, and there's Campbell in the stands. He never shows up at Lakeland. I just knew instinctively he was there to fire me. And that would be the end. So I walked up to him and said: 'Jim, I won't let you fire me. This isn't fair. You're not giving me a chance. I won't let you do it.' Then I turned around and walked away.

"Years later, when I was inducted into the Canadian Sports Hall of Fame, Jim got up and spoke and said that I was right. He had come down to release me, but when he saw how determined I was he changed his mind. So by that much I was saved.

"I finally got in to see that heart specialist, and he gave me the exam, and then he just sat back and winked at me. 'Be patient,' he said. That was it. Be patient. Well, I figured I couldn't live like this anymore, so I flew back to Duluth and asked about getting my department store job back. That's when Campbell called. 'Get down to Chicago,' he told me. 'Let's see how you can throw.'

"I was throwing the ball harder than I ever had in my life. Losing that weight seemed to make my fastball move better than before. Two of Detroit's relievers had gotten hurt, and it was between me and Les Cain, who'd been having some arm troubles, as to who would make the team. That's what Billy Martin decided. We'd go into the bull pen, and whoever threw best got the job. I don't want to be irreverent or anything, but they could have put Jesus Christ on the mound next to me, and I'd have out-thrown him. After what I'd been through, no way I wouldn't get that job.

"Next day, they put me in the game. Dick Allen is the hitter. He looks at a fastball. He looks at a curve. Then he looks at me as if to say: 'OK, is that what you've got?' I throw another curve-ball, and he puts into the left-field roof at Comiskey Park. Not on the roof. That thing was still rising when it hit the bottom side. It put a dent in the metal. And I say to myself: 'Holy jeez, this is what I came back for?' But I came back, threw three more innings with no runs and no walks.

"That's when Martin tells the clubhouse: 'What's the matter with you guys? Here's Hiller back from the dead, and he can throw strikes. Why can't you?'"

Hiller went on to pitch twenty-four times for the division champions and threw three innings of shutout relief in the play-offs. In 1973, used entirely as a closer, he saved thirty-eight games, establishing a major league record. In the first five years after his comeback his ERA was never higher than 2.64.

"Billy was throwing me in practically every day," he says. "Once he made me go sit in the clubhouse instead of going to the bull pen, but he called me out of there and brought me in the game anyhow. Next day he told me to stay at the hotel. He couldn't get me in the game from there.

"I was the last one from the old bunch. I stayed until 1980, and then I felt I just wasn't doing the job, and I quit. I mean why should I take the ball club's salary when I couldn't earn it anymore? The Tigers didn't owe me a thing. I gave them everything I had as a player, but I'd have done the same thing if I'd pitched for Boston or Cleveland or anyone. It's the only way I knew how to play. I always felt maybe they could take more advantage of us from a public relations standpoint. But once I walked out of that clubhouse as a player, that was it. It wasn't my clubhouse anymore. I never went back."

Hiller has kept off most of his weight—and most of his hair, too. He's been a moderate drinker since the heart attack, lives simply. The wild days of '68 are a long time ago and far, far away.

"They're always on the phone with me to work autograph shows," he says. "I can't do it. Not unless it's a charitable thing. I tried it once, and I felt like a whore. All these little kids paying to get in so I could give them my autograph. I can't do that.

"When I was playing, the old-timers would come into the clubhouse and talk about how they don't play the game like they used to. I always told myself I'd never be like that. But you know the old saying: Money changes everything. It's all different now. The first little pain, and they're on the disabled list. I see guys on TV laughing on the bench when they're ten runs down. God, Billy Martin would've killed 'em. Hey, we gave our lives for a paycheck, and it was a good game back then. I just can't get very interested in it anymore."

◊

When the *1968 Tigers season opened, Detroit was still reeling from the previous summer's riots, which destroyed many homes—and shook the confidence of the city. In the summer to come, the tensions responsible for the '67 mayhem, gave way to new tensions: rooting for the Tigers.*

The Tiger brass: General Manager Jim Campbell, owner John Fetzer, and Manager Mayo Smith. They put together the '68 Tigers.

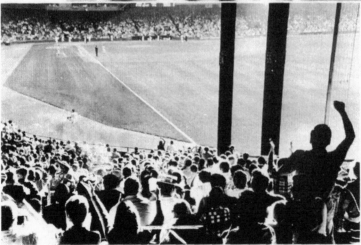

Al Kaline and his "Corner." The 1968 season marked the only World Series appearance for the future Hall of Famer, who was viewed with such reverence by the organization that they reconfigured their ballpark in the early sixties (by removing seats down the right-field line that Kaline regularly crashed into) and their lineup for the '68 series so Kaline could play.

First baseman Norm Cash was easily the most popular member of the Tigers in the clubhouse—and after hours. He kept the team loose and balanced all season.

Third baseman Don Wert was not flashy, but he did provide stability at an important position.

Reliever Pat Dobson recorded seven saves, tied for the team lead. He would go on to win twenty games for Baltimore in 1971, becoming one of four twenty-game winners on the Birds' staff that year.

Former Ohio State quarterback Joe Sparma pitched the pennant-clinching game on September 17. It was a rare highlight in his career, one of generally unfulfilled promise.

Pitcher Earl Wilson was one of only two Tigers starters who began his career with another organization (Norm Cash was the other). Earl was also one of only three blacks on the team and the only one from the South. His 2.85 ERA was second best among the starters, but he suffered a loss in his sole appearance in the series.

Outfielder and slugger Willie Horton grew up in Detroit and enjoyed the unwavering support of the city's fans, who viewed Willie as one of them.

John Hiller was a spot starter and reliever in 1968. Following a massive heart attack at a young age in 1971 (he was 27), he fought his way back to become the Tigers all-time saves leader. He was also the last member of the '68 Tigers to leave the team.

Tommy Matchick, a lightly regarded utility infielder, was the unlikely hero the night of July 19, an electric evening when Matchick hit a two-out, two-run homer in the bottom of the ninth against the Orioles to give the Tigers an improbable 5-4 win. The comeback was emblematic of the season, when it seemed as if every game was decided with ninth-inning heroics.

If Kaline was the soul of the '68 Tigers, catcher Bill Freehan was the glue. A perennial all-star, Freehan was a Michigan native who anchored the infield and called near flawless games behind the plate.

Gates Brown's bottom-of-the-ninth pinch hit beats Boston 6-5 on August 11. It capped an unforgettable day for Gates, who had lifted the Tigers to a 5-4 win in the first game of the doubleheader with a pinch-hit homer in the fourteenth. Such moments belonged to the Gater, who hit .462 as a pinch hitter in 1968.

Scrappy Dick McAuliffe, who blossomed after Mayo Smith moved him from shortstop to second base, was, as leadoff man, the key to the Tigers' offense. The Tigers lost four of the five games McAuliffe missed due to his suspension for charging Chicago pitcher Tommy John after John buzzed McAuliffe with a couple of pitches. An injury sustained during the melee put John out for the season.

Denny McLain returns to acknowledge the fans, who chanted "We want Denny," after he won his thirtieth game on September 14. McLain was the first thirty-game winner since 1934, when Dizzy Dean, who was on hand for the game, went 30-7. McLain one upped Dean by finishing 31-6.

Mickey Mantle's second-to-last career home run came off McLain at Tiger Stadium on September 19, 1968. It was probably the surest shot of his career. With the pennant in the bag and the Tigers leading 6-1, McLain, as a "tribute" to the Mick, tipped off Mantle as to where his next pitch would be. After fouling off that pitch in disbelief, Mantle played along, indicating where he wanted the next pitch. McLain obliged and Mantle hit it into the right-field stands for home run number 535.

...eworks salute the champions of the American League, who clinched the pennant in typical dramatic fashion ... the night of September 17.

To open a World Series spot for Al Kaline in the crowded Tigers outfield, the usually conservative Mayo Smith made a bold move, replacing good-field, absolutely no-hit (how 'bout .135?) shortstop Ray Oyler (right) with Gold Glove centerfielder Mickey Stanley (above).

The World Series opened ominously for the Tigers as Lou Brock cracked a homer off Pat Dobson and ran wild on the bases, and Bob Gibson struck out a series record seventeen batters.

Bill Freehan blocks Lou Brock away from the plate in game five's pivotal play and the series' turning point.

Jim Northrup is greeted by his team-mates after belting a grand slam to highlight the Tigers' ten-run third inning in game six. It was Northrup's fifth slam of the year, leading Ernie Harwell to give The Silver Fox a new nickname, "The Slammer."

Mickey Lolich emerged from McLain's shadow by winning three games in the '68 World Series, including game seven when he beat the seemingly unbeatable Bob Gibson.

Twenty-three years of emptiness about to end as Bill Freehan waits for Tim McCarver's foul pop fly to land safely in his mitt for the last out of the 1968 World Series.

Detroit cuts loose—this time out of joy.

SUNNY

METRO
Stocks Lose
Trading Heavy
See Page 10, Section B

Detroit Free Press
ON GUARD FOR 137 YEARS

Vol. 138—No. 159 Friday, October 11, 1968 Ten Cents

JIM NORTHRUP

WE WIN!

MICKEY LOLICH

City Goes Wild After Tiger Victory

Action Line
Dial 222-6464

Action Line solves problems, gets answers, cuts red tape, speeds up for your rights. Write Action Line, Box 881, Detroit, Mich. 48231. Or dial 222-6464 between 8:30 a.m. and 4:40 p.m. Monday through Friday.

BY BARBARA STANTON
Free Press Staff Writer

Detroit went hell-bent for a hangover Thursday night in raucous, rowdy triumph after the Tigers won the World Series.

World champions!

At 4:06 p.m., Bill Freehan caught a pop fly in St. Louis and Detroit exploded like a magnificent firecracker.

People poured into the streets, confetti rained from the heavens, horns rang, and whistles and squeals and sirens rose in one great, gorgeous, swelling sound until hearts burst from the joy of it.

Suddenly nothing would ever be impossible again.

The unbelievable, unpredictable Tigers had done it.

Rin Tin Tin, was a German shepherd.

AND A TROPHY TO PROVE IT! Exuberant Dick McAuliffe, left, with Jim Northrup, center, and Mickey Stanley left it all as they display the trophy that goes to baseball's World Champions.

Tigers Avoid Welcoming Mob

Our Man in the Bleachers

The Big Victory

George Cantor's story of the Tigers' triumph. Page 1D.

Dick Mayer's World Series, Page 3A.

Violence and vandalism mar Tiger celebration. Page 4B.

Mickey Lolich's mother has "never worried about him—even today." Page 1C.

More pictures on Page 11C and Back Page.

The Champions Weep in Joy

BY BOB TALBERT
Free Press Columnist

Inside the Free Press

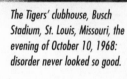

The Tigers' clubhouse, Busch Stadium, St. Louis, Missouri, the evening of October 10, 1968: disorder never looked so good.

To the victors go the spoils.

CHAPTER 21

Laughing All the Way

In the streets of Chicago, the nation seemed to be fighting for its sanity. The Democratic Convention had gathered for the business of nominating Hubert H. Humphrey for president. Antiwar demonstrators, infuriated by what they perceived to be nothing more than a continuation of American policy in Vietnam, turned the city into a gypsy camp and then into a battleground. For three days, city cops were pelted with words, garbage, and abuse. Then, with the blessing of Mayor Richard Daley, police struck back. Young demonstrators were clubbed, gassed, pursued into hotels, and beaten. Senator Abraham Ribicoff stood on the convention podium and berated Daley. The mayor cursed him right back, and it seemed that democracy itself was going to split wide open in a free-for-all.

The Tigers saw very little of that from the bus. Although Comiskey Park was just a few miles from the site of the convention, it all could have been happening in Prague—where Soviet troops were on the march, stamping out the last faint embers of Czech democracy.

Never was the distance between the drumbeat of reality and the unchanging rhythm of baseball wider than in these last days of August. The Tigers were too occupied with trying to put their world back together to notice the planet coming apart. They were facing their own private upheaval after the fiasco in New York. As during the riot that took place behind the left-field wall in Detroit one year ago, they could smell the smoke. But the fire never touched them.

The first game with the White Sox had been switched from Chicago to Milwaukee. The Democrats had booked all the hotel rooms in the Chicago area, and the White Sox had also agreed to play nine home games in the nearby city. Milwaukee had lost its Braves to Atlanta after the 1965 season, and there was some speculation that the Sox would move to the Wisconsin city. At the very least, they were keeping it warm until another ball club arrived. The Detroit game drew almost 43,000 people, the largest Milwaukee crowd of the year.

The team plane had arrived from New York after midnight, and the Tigers disembarked in relief. The temperature was twenty degrees cooler, the humidity was down. Earl Wilson, scheduled to pitch that night, decided to "do things right" and never went to bed. Then he went out and pitched a six-hit shutout and drove in the first two runs of the 3–0 win. Even though Detroit lost the next night in Chicago, there was a strong feeling among the Tigers that the worst was behind them. They had been through the fire and survived. McAuliffe would be back in the lineup when they got home. McLain would open the series against California, trying once more for victory number twenty-six. Everyone was certain that he would not fail a third time.

But the operative word was "home." The 1968 Tigers were Michigan's team in every sense. Four of their regulars had come out of the state, giving the team an unusually strong identification with its home base. The Yankee dynasty had been over for just four years. It crumbled for many reasons. But one of the most basic was the initiation of the player draft. Teams could no longer sign and stockpile the best talent for any price they chose to pay. The day of the "bonus baby" and the deep farm system stocked with a decade's worth of talent were over. Now there was equity. Since the collapse of the Yankees, three different teams had won a pennant, and the Tigers would soon make it four. The last time that had happened in the American League was 1943-46, and it took a world war to bring it about. Prior to that you had to go back to 1918-21, at the very dawn of the Yankee era, to find a similar balance.

But something had also been lost. The draft made it almost impossible for a team to sign the top local players. The era in which players actually had a hometown bond with the area in which they performed had ended. Even the lordly Yankees always seemed to have a Lou Gehrig and a Waite Hoyt, a Phil Rizzuto and a Whitey Ford—kids who had learned the game on the streets of the big city. Now the players came from anywhere.

But this Detroit team was a vestige of earlier times. Willie Horton, from the city's sandlots. Bill Freehan, from the suburbs and the University of Michigan. Jim Northrup, from Alma College. Mickey Stanley, from the state's second city, Grand Rapids. It seemed that everyone in Michigan knew someone who knew them personally. There was an identification with them throughout the state as "our team," and that would never be duplicated in the future.

Sparma, Brown, Warden, McLain, Oyler, Lasher, Hiller—all of them came from neighboring states in the same part of the country (or, in Hiller's case, the adjacent corner of Canada). Tracewski, Matchick, and Price grew up in Pennsylvania indus-trial towns that weren't all that different. This geographic coherence produced a profound similarity of outlook, an innate understanding of who each other was. It was a strong unifying influence. Players shared a view of the world and how to have fun in it.

Maybe the most notorious shared caper of this team was the Plane in the Pool. It has passed into team legend as the epitome of what hard work, teamplay, and a certain degree of strong waters can achieve.

The Tigers had first seen the wooden replica of an antique aircraft in the lobby of their hotel in Anaheim as they checked in for the start of the series. A convention of aviation enthusiasts was also booked into the hotel. The players always had time on their hands in Anaheim. The hotel was right across the road from Disneyland, but that paled after the first few visits. There was no shopping or movies nearby. Not a lot to do but watch TV, play cards, and think deep thoughts. It turned out that the plane was on a lot of the Tigers' minds.

After night games in Anaheim most of the players would repair to the nightclub on the top floor of the hotel. It was a favorite hangout. The team had welcomed the start of the 1967 season with a gala party there. Oyler had become so gala at this party that he had to be carried out feet first on the eve of his debut as Detroit's regular shortstop. In spite of this, he still managed to go hitless. The celebration on this occasion was a bit less jolly, and some of the players were looking for a way to liven up things. That's when the idea of removing the plane from the lobby and taking it to the hotel's outdoor swimming pool first was suggested.

An advance scouting party reported back that there were a few problems. The plane was too big to fit through the door to the pool. It would have to be disassembled. Moreover, it was situated uncomfortably close to the front desk. The night clerk couldn't see it, but he might be able to hear. Precautions would have to be taken. Moreover, this was especially risky business because Campbell was on this road trip. Usually, when reports of misbehavior trickled back to him a few days after the fact, he would angrily erupt, but time and distance usually eased his displeasure. With him right on the scene, there was an added element of danger.

"I still don't know where they came up with the tools," says Lolich, fondly recalling the event like a general of a great war. "But we had some very resourceful guys on that team. When I saw the tools I knew it could be done. I always loved to tinker with stuff when I was a kid, taking things apart and putting them back together. The plane would be a cinch. So we sent Hiller out to the lobby as a diversionary tactic. He got the desk clerk, who was half asleep anyhow, into a conversation about baseball. Hiller was told to talk loud so the rest of us could get to work on the plane."

Within twenty minutes, these highly skilled athletes had taken the plane apart and noiselessly transported it to the pool area, where it was reassembled. Then the players gathered to admire their night's work. But something was missing, the finishing touch that would elevate this escapade above the routine. No one will take credit for what happened next. All those named as the culpable party are no longer living. But someone decided that the next logical step was to put the plane into the pool.

"It surprised us how easily it went in," says Lolich. "We slid it to the side, but then it got a little tricky, because we didn't want it to make too big a splash when it hit the water. So we kind of lowered it and then just let go."

Unfortunately, the Tigers had forgotten their basic Archimedean physics. When the plane went into the pool, an equal weight of water had to come out. "One minute we were standing there," says Lolich, "admiring the plane in the pool, and the next we were caught in a flood. The whole pool area went underwater. We had to turn around and run like hell."

One of their rooms overlooked the pool, and the Tigers scurried up there to see the total effect of what they had done. The plane, which had settled to the pool floor, presented a lovely spectacle in the moonlight. To Lolich it was one of the transcendental moments of his life with the Tigers.

"The hotel knew who had done it right away," he says. "They had to. We were all waiting the next day for the explosion from Campbell. But it never came. We found out later that he had just settled privately with the hotel and paid for the damage. He never said a word."

Maybe that was because the general manager had been in the U.S. Naval Air Corps in World War II and the incident brought back fond memories. More likely, Cambell just wanted to keep the whole thing hushed up and out of the newspapers, where it would have landed in big print if he had handed out fines.

But now it was time for the Tigers to have the last laugh.

CHAPTER 22

Rolling to 30

When the Tigers ran onto the field to play California on the evening of August 28, their lead had shriveled to a mere four games. That was as small as it had been since June 11. So Detroit's fans turned out with some trepidation to watch the latest turn that the drama would take. They would see, instead, the curtain rise on the final act. The Tigers were about to take off on a 19–4 spurt that would feature some of the most remarkable events in the history of the franchise.

McLain began it by notching win twenty-six, an effortless six-hitter, with Freehan and Northrup pounding big home runs in a 6–1 game. Then it was Lolich's turn. After returning from his exile to the bull pen (in which he'd won three games in five days), the left-hander finally looked like the Lolich who had finished the 1967 season. He stopped the Angels 2–0, giving up no hits after the second and mowing down the last twenty hitters in a row. It was his strongest game of the year, and several Tigers observed that he now seemed to be throwing the ball better than McLain.

Then it was Baltimore's turn. Before a capacity Friday night crowd, Wilson pitched a four-hitter, crashed a three-run homer, and cruised home to a 9–1 win. The Orioles came back behind Dave McNally on Saturday. This set up the ultimate confrontation on Sunday.

It would be Baltimore's last chance to cut into Detroit's lead until the final week of the season. The Orioles had no qualms about facing McLain. Twenty-six wins or no, they had handled him well, dealing him two of his five losses this year. The games were not squeakers, either. His losses to Baltimore were the only games in which he failed to last until at least the fifth inning. The Orioles would also oppose him with their top winner, Jim Hardin.

It was the day before Labor Day in the final all-or-nothing September pennant race in major league history. In 1969, four teams would get into the new playoff format. That number was expanded to eight in 1995. But in 1968 there was no margin for error, no second chance. If a team stumbled in September, there could be no October revival. Nothing could save it. Only the winners reached the World Series. So when two top contenders met in September, the sport reached its pinnacle. This game was to be the last of its kind.

Before the crowd could get settled in, Curt Blefary cracked a two-run homer, and Baltimore was off to a 2–0 lead. But Northrup matched that homer when the Tigers came to bat. Then they drove out Hardin with two more in the second and carried a 4–2 lead into the third.

McLain's control had been remarkable all year. But he began this inning by walking Don Buford. Blefary and Frank Robinson followed with singles, and now it was 4–3. Two runners on, and the fearsome Boog Powell (the blond giant whom Cash referred to as "Moby Dick") was coming to the plate. The crowd understood that the season had reached, at last, its defining moment. This is where the best pitcher in baseball had to walk the walk.

Powell swung, and the ball was a blur. For an instant, no one could follow where it went. Then suddenly McLain was whirling around on the mound, the ball in his hand, firing toward second. Matchick took the throw at the bag and relayed it to first.

Triple play.

In an instant, Powell's screaming line drive right back at McLain had been transformed into the bolt that broke the Orioles.

Bill Wambsganns, who turned the unassisted triple play in the 1920 World Series, spoke afterward of the dead calm that covered Cleveland's League Park as he trotted off the field. The crowd couldn't absorb what it had just witnessed. Only several seconds later did the ovation roll like thunder from the stands. That's how it was in Detroit on this Sunday. The Tigers left the field in a web of stunned silence. As they reached the dugout, the crowd exploded, understanding that they had just seen the beginning of the end. The season had been sealed with this trifecta.

McLain gave up two meaningless singles the rest of the way, and the Tigers eased off with a 7–3 win. The lead was now seven games, and Baltimore would never again come any closer than that.

But Denny was not content. Now 27–5, with a month still to play, he felt compelled to give the play an even larger meaning.

"The ball was heading right at my head," he told reporters in the clubhouse. "If I hadn't caught it, it would've killed me."

So it wasn't just a triple play. It was a Death-Defying Triple Play. It was the Mother of All Triple Plays.

Only when photos ran in the papers the following day was it apparent that McLain actually had caught the ball around his belt buckle. It was still a nice play, and it would have been a painful event had he missed. But not quite the fatal impact that Denny was proclaiming.

No matter. The caravan rolled on.

Number twenty-eight came against the Twins, with Horton driving in five runs in a rather easy 8–3 win.

Number twenty-nine was in Anaheim. Lolich had pitched a two-hit shutout the night before. But it was McLain whom the fans wanted to see.

This time it was the full-bore Hollywood treatment. Singer Glen Campbell was his guest in the clubhouse. Tommy Smothers, at the height of his popularity with the irreverent *Smothers Brothers* TV show, had McLain out to his house. Ed Sullivan paid a call to line up McLain for his show. An introduction on a Sunday night *Ed Sullivan Show* still represented the ultimate in celebrity for an American hero. Almost incidentally, McLain disposed of the Angels 7–2 for win number twenty-nine, getting three hits himself, including a triple.

On Saturday, September 14, he started against Oakland at Tiger Stadium and went for number thirty.

The race was just about over. Detroit now matched its largest lead of the year, 9½ games. But this game was covered as if it meant the pennant. Reporters from most major newspapers and weekly magazines were in the press box. So was Dizzy Dean, the last man to win thirty, hired by the *Detroit News* to write his observations on the historic event. At least Dean was in the press box for a while. The president of the Detroit chapter of the Baseball Writers Association of America decreed that Dean did not have the proper credentials to get a seat in this hallowed journalism sanctuary. Because the president was also the baseball writer for the *News*, his decree was all the more embarrassing. Dean was removed to the auxiliary box and had to be content to observe history from there.

This was also the nationally televised Game of the Week, and the network brought in Sandy Koufax as its commentator. Retired for two seasons, Koufax, the greatest pitcher of his time, had won as many as twenty-seven. But no more than that. So McLain would make his effort in the presence of greatness.

The As were a young team, just starting to assemble the core that would win three consecutive championships in the early '70s. Reggie Jackson was already in the lineup. So were Bert

Campaneris, Sal Bando, and Dick Green, while future Hall of Famers Catfish Hunter and Rollie Fingers were on the pitching staff. The As were still three years away from winning their first division title, only one year from the last of several last-place finishes in Kansas City. They strongly desired not to be Denny's thirtieth. During batting practice one of the As attached a sign to his uniform that read: "Watch Chuck Dobson go for number twelve today." It was a pointed reminder that Oakland did not intend to go quietly into the record book.

Jackson was especially cranked up for this game. He was in his first full season in the majors, already marked for stardom. The situation stirred the competitive fires that in another decade would win him the title of "Mr. October." In the fourth he took McLain upstairs in right field, and Oakland was away to a 2–0 lead. But Cash trumped it in the home half with a three-run shot, and McLain had his lead.

But he couldn't hold it. Campaneris tied the score with a single in the fifth, and soon after Jackson came up and crushed another one, this time with the bases empty. The As were back in front, 4–3. Meanwhile, Diego Segui entered the game in the fifth and stymied the Tigers, shutting them down on three singles as the game entered the ninth.

The official attendance at this game was only 33,686, but the park was filled much closer to its capacity. The Tigers traditionally gave away 10,000 tickets as a gesture of goodwill to Detroit schools for Saturday games in September. This one, despite its significance, was no exception. The tickets had been handed out months before. The entire left-field lower deck was occupied by screaming safety patrol boys, on a free pass to one of the most historic ball games in Detroit history. In most moments of high drama, the sound level in a big-league ballpark is like a low roar. But the noise on this day was more like a continuous screech, the shrill battle cry one might have heard at the Children's Crusade.

Kaline led off the ninth inning as a pinch hitter for McLain. It was becoming increasingly difficult for Mayo to find spots for his veteran star. The manager was reluctant to break up the young outfield combination that was winning a pennant for him. Cash had started to hit steadily at first base. Kaline had been relegated to the role of occasional player and pinch hitter. On this assignment, he worked Segui for a walk.

With the national media assembled to watch McLain reach his milestone, it would have been a bum scenario for him to stumble and then have to try all over again in four more days. Neither Denny nor the Tigers were into anticlimax this season. With McLain out of the game, they had to win it in this inning.

McAuliffe popped up, but Stanley sent a single to center, advancing Kaline, the consummate baserunner, to third. Kaline's ability to take the extra base forced Oakland to draw in its infield to cut down the tying run at the plate. That set up what happened next.

Northrup sent a harmless hopper toward first baseman Danny Cater. Kaline broke for the plate on contact, and it appeared that he would be out easily. But this play was like so many others during this season. In critical moments, something odd would occur. Cater led all first basemen in the league in fielding, committing merely five errors all year. This was number five. He rushed his throw to the plate, and catcher Dave Duncan had to reach back for it just as Kaline came plowing into him. The ball sailed past them both. Kaline touched the plate on his hands and knees, while Stanley went all the way to third.

It was happening again. The winning run was now at third, as the youth corps in the left-field seats implored its hero, Horton, to bring it home. The As had to bring in the outfield for the play at the plate. Horton sent a long fly to left. Even with the fielder in normal position it would have scored the run as a sacrifice fly. Now it fell safely over the leftfielder's head for a single, and Stanley raced home with win number thirty.

Kaline was standing next to McLain in the dugout when Horton's ball went over the outfielder's head. As he grabbed McLain in an uncharacteristically emotional embrace (which made the cover of *Sports Illustrated*) the two went rushing onto the field in tandem. The Tigers descended on Stanley at home and then ran out to get Horton, trotting back toward the baseline. Despite what they might have felt about McLain personally, they knew that they were touching history at this moment, that they had become a part of the game's legend.

Then something even more unusual happened. The crowd refused to leave. The entire throng, safety boys and all, stood at its seats and started to chant. "We want Denny. We want Denny." McLain, by this time, was already surrounded by media in the clubhouse. Even in there, deep under the stands, you could hear the feet pounding and the distant cheers. Public relations director Hal Middlesworth burst into the clubhouse. Usually the calmest of men, Middlesworth rushed up to McLain, interrupting the interviews. "You're going to have to go out there," he told him. "They're not going to leave."

In subsequent years, the curtain call from the dugout, the reappearance on the field of the player who has performed memorably, has become a part of baseball. It occurred at its most moving when Cal Ripken Jr. broke the consecutive game record in 1995 and took his walk of triumph around Camden Yards. But in the late '60s, such displays were unknown. Ballplayers finished their heroics on the field and then left the premises. Coming back out to wave and blow kisses would have been dismissed as showboating.

So when McLain walked back down the tunnel and climbed out of the dugout to wave at the frenzied throng it was a moment unprecedented in Detroit and rare in the entire game. Koufax, tagging right behind him with a TV camera crew, kept looking around and repeating: "Isn't this incredible. Isn't this just incredible." The veteran of four World Series had never seen anything like it.

McLain walked slowly around the perimeter of the infield, waving his cap. For once even he didn't seem to know what to do, how to handle this display of love and emotion. If he had called out: "Enough with the noise; throw out your wallets," they would have done that, too. Just four months ago he had called them the worst fans in the world. All forgotten now.

Then he was back in the clubhouse, posing for pictures with the exuberant Dean. "I'm just proud to play with that man," said Horton at his locker. "We were in the minor leagues together, and now we're here. I'm proud to know him."

But there were even prouder moments to come.

CHAPTER 23

End of the Weight

There had been pennant waits longer than twenty-three years. Much longer. Even in the history of the Detroit franchise, the gap between the pennants of 1909 and 1934 exceeded this gap by two years. Of the original sixteen major league teams, only three—the Yankees, Dodgers, and Reds—would never wait longer between pennants. A few teams would wait more than forty seasons, the Cubs over fifty.

What had made this wait so acute for Detroit's fans was that they had never watched their team win on TV. The revolution in communications since 1945 had skipped right over the Tigers. Watching the team you root for play on network TV, seen by the entire nation, seemed to validate your experience as a fan. Television brought an immediacy to sports unlike anything that had gone before. It had become the stamp of reality. Just as when McLain took his bow on the *Ed Sullivan Show*, being on national television was the mark of genuine celebrity. But for Detroit's postwar generation, who grew up with a TV set as part of the family, it was always somebody else's team being shown. The wait of twenty-three years seemed longer than it actually was because in that span every one of the other original teams, except the Cubs and As, had taken their turn on the tube.

Then there was the unresolved matter of '67. It still hung like a thundercloud over the heads of the Tigers and Detroit. The pennant blown and the chance squandered. The fires of July. The memory of the terrible events of the past year still shrouded the city like an evil mist. Although that mist would never entirely dissipate, there is nothing else in sports quite like a pennant race. The day-by-day immersion in its drama, the addition of a new chapter at every sunset, each new twist to the tale. Baseball draws its acolytes in like a soap opera with spikes. While the story continues, other concerns recede. That is how it was in Detroit in the summer of 1968. Some called it a healing, but it was more like a disease had gone into deep remission.

Three days after McLain's thirtieth, the last number came up for the Tigers. The number was one, the final Detroit win or Baltimore loss needed to reach the Magic Moment. The *Free Press* had received hundreds of thousands of entries for its pro-motion. As the hour approached, those who had chosen September 17 as the date gathered around their radios to hear the clock strike.

It was Wilson's turn in the rotation. But as he warmed up in the left-field bull pen to face the Yankees, something didn't feel right in his shoulder. He mentioned it to Sain, and Mayo immediately decided to make a switch. Joe Sparma, who hadn't won a game in almost two months, was told to start throwing.

Since his tiff with the manager in early August, Sparma had been forgotten. He was only 8–10 for the season and deeply wounded in his soul. While his contemporaries, the other Boys from Syracuse, were winning the pennant, Sparma remained out-side the baselines, given nothing to do and no promise for the future. Confused and depressed, he watched the season pass as if it were happening to someone else.

This call was a rush job, and he had no chance to let the situation get to him mentally. He was given a few extra minutes to warm up because of the injury to Wilson and then just thrown right into it. He almost washed right out of it, too. He gave up two hits in the first and only a double play got him out of the inning. After that he was untouchable. Through the eighth, he allowed just one more hit and faced the minimum of twenty-one hitters. The only two Yankees to get on were thrown out by Freehan on steal attempts. This was the Sparma the Tigers had seen in their dreams. Ahead in the count, in command of his breaking pitches, unable to be pulled. Moreover, when the Tigers scored a run in the fifth, it was Sparma who cashed it in with a single up the middle.

The crowd of 46,000, the last big one of the regular season, began screaming in anticipation as the ninth began. It had been a fast game. Sparma walked only one man and hadn't struck out anyone. The Magic Moment looked as if it would strike shortly before 10:00 P.M., Detroit time.

But pinch hitter Charley Smith led off with a single, and two outs later he had advanced to second. With the crowd howling on each pitch, Jake Gibbs lined a single, and the game was suddenly tied. In the ensuing silence, a disgusted Sparma pounded his glove, stomped around on the mound, and then came back to strike out Mantle. Now the Tigers would have to clinch the pennant in their half of the inning.

But they already had. At 9:58 P.M., six hundred miles to the east in Fenway Park, the Red Sox got the last out in a 2–0 win over the Orioles. The race was over. In an odd reversal of the previous year, in which the Red Sox had waited in their clubhouse for the news that the Tigers had lost in Detroit, the Tigers found that they had won by the word out of Boston.

But the word never made it to the Tiger Stadium scoreboard. Campbell feared that posting the result could trigger a demonstration that would make the rest of this game unplayable. So as the twenty-three-year wait ended, the Tigers soldiered on in the dark. Hiller, sitting in the clubhouse because he had pitched the night before, heard the news on television. Racing down the tunnel to the bench he started to yell. "Guys, it's over. We've won." Mayo practically jumped on top of him, telling him to shut up. He wanted his team to win it on their own. Only a few of the Tigers heard what Hiller had said. They said nothing more about it. Observers could detect no trace of emotion on the bench.

For a while, it looked as if Campbell would have to keep the lid on the news for a long time. Reliever Steve Hamilton got the first two hitters in the ninth easily. Then Kaline was called on to pinch-hit. When he'd left home that morning, he told his wife, Louise, he had the feeling that he was going to do something big in the game. It was not the sort of thing he had ever mentioned before. But sitting on the bench was a baffling, unsettling experience for Kaline. Never in his career had he been relegated to this kind of role. He was unprepared for it and, like Sparma, waited impatiently for a chance at redemption.

Just as he had a few days before, at the start of the rally for McLain's thirtieth, Kaline drew a walk. Freehan then singled to left, and the Yankees changed pitchers, bringing in Lindy McDaniel to face pinch hitter Price. Mayo responded by calling for Gates Brown, and McDaniel, pitching carefully, walked him to load the bases. That brought up Wert.

The sad-faced little third baseman was not having a good year as a hitter. He had averaged .255 in his first five seasons with the Tigers. But now he was having a hard time staying above .200, although remaining a rock of consistency at third base. Uncomplaining, always laughing quietly at the strange behavior going on all around him, Wert was regarded with deep affection by his teammates. He was "Coyote," the name Don Demeter had come up with for him several years ago in an effort to draw the shy rookie within the circle of the team. Demeter said that something in Wert's eyes reminded him of the animals he saw on his Oklahoma ranch.

Now the crowd was up again, pleading for the hit that would win it. Wert swung late and sent a looper toward the right side. In an instant, everyone saw that it would clear Horace Clarke's glove and land safely in the outfield. Before Kaline could fulfill the prophecy he had made to his wife hours before and score the run that, apparently, would win the pennant, the first wave of spectators came over the top of the stands.

Campbell's fears had been well founded. As the Tigers hurriedly congratulated each other and then rushed into the clubhouse in a bellowing mob, the fans took over the field, tearing up turf and bases and anything else that could be lifted for a souvenir.

This, too, was not customary behavior in 1968. In the early years of the twentieth century, when spectators were allowed to stand behind ropes in the outfield for big games, crowd control was a bit of a problem. But those days were long gone. Even in the most dramatic victories, crowds refrained from coming onto the playing surface. That was sacred ground. But this was the '60s, and nothing was sacred. By the mid '70s, teams routinely had to post police guards, some of them mounted, around the field to stop such celebrations before they got rolling.

Although the Tigers expected some disturbance, they never anticipated this. They had made no arrangements for added security. Instead, they ordered fireworks. The lights were turned off and illuminated bursts were sent soaring high above the center-field scoreboard. Through the rockets' red glare, you could see the fans methodically tearing up the field, like a pageant reen-acting the fall of the Bastille. The revelry didn't end until the fireworks concluded, with the message "Sock It To 'Em, Tigers" emblazoned across the night sky. Only then did guards finally go onto the field to roust the remaining pockets of joy.

There was also madness in the clubhouse—the traditional champagne-spewing, whirlpool-dunking, cigar-chomping cele-bration. Mathews and Roy Face, acquired from Pittsburgh in the last two weeks of the season as the final bit of pennant insurance, watched the wildness unfold before them, nudging each other to draw attention to some of the more bizarre antics. They had been through it before. This time they were content to observe.

Many of the Tigers, never slow to accept a glass, were slumped by their lockers, broad grins spreading over their vacant faces. In the entire room, only Wert sat upright in front of his locker. He held a beer in his hand. A small smile was on his face. Surrounded by the massive egos and large personalities around him, he was content to perch all by himself and reflect upon what he had set off with one swing of his bat. A wily Coyote, finally getting the best of a roomful of Roadrunners. But for all of the Tigers, the wait was over, and the weight had finally been lifted from their backs.

In the city, the party spread down Michigan Avenue from the stadium to the streets of downtown. Crowds lined up ten deep in front of the Lindell A.C., trying to get in to toast the moment. Attorney Fred Steinhardt, just out of law school, was one of the lucky few who managed to squeeze inside. "It was the party of the century," he recalls. "Everybody laughing, singing. At one point, Lolich and McLain wound up behind the bar giving away drinks for free. I still had the feeling that the World Series—who knows? It might all end there. But the pennant was ours. Whatever happened it was ours to keep. So we had to celebrate."

Thousands of others were content to walk down the avenues, beers in their hands, howling at the sky. Every street was like Mardi Gras that night. It was after 11:00 P.M. on a Tuesday night. But the streets of Detroit, long deserted in the months after the previous July's riots, were packed again with happy people.

Wells Twombley had just been hired by the *Free Press* as its pro football writer. He had worked late in the office, putting this monumental edition of the sports page to bed. Then he joined a group of other writers to walk to a nearby bar. For some reason, Twombley was offended by the merriment breaking out all around him. As one reveler walked by, shouting wildly to no one in particular, Twombley shoved him and told him to shut up. The cheerful fan turned around and punched his lights out. Twombley crumpled to the pavement and hit the side of his head on the curb. The incident left him with a permanent hearing impairment. It was, however, one of the few reports of violence that evening.

One other such incident came in the hospitality room at Tiger

Stadium. Yankee manager Ralph Houk had been ejected from the game and was not in the best of moods. He also had been angered earlier in the week by an article in *The Sporting News* that contrasted the success of the Detroit farm system to that of the Yankees. Houk, who had stepped down as general manager, took this as a personal affront. When Houk found that the author of the article, Tom Loomis of the *Toledo Blade*, was in the room, he sought out Loomis and began to yell at him. Then he went at Loomis and had to be pulled off by his coaches. It was an odd end to the pennant celebration at the ballpark.

There was, however, one last bit of business to attend to before the World Series. It was Denny's final moment—his last chance to be ringmaster, lion tamer, and acrobat all at once. The game after the pennant clincher was rained out, an act of divine intercession because it was doubtful that enough sober Tigers could have been rounded up to play. Even with McLain starting the next day, fewer than 10,000 fans found their way to the ballpark for the last game with the Yankees.

Once again, McLain was in complete command as he went for win number thirty-one. Cash hit a couple of homers, and going into the eighth McLain was coasting with a 6–1 lead. With one out, Mantle started walking to the plate for what most people assumed would be his final time at bat at Tiger Stadium. It was widely rumored that he would soon announce his retirement. But for reasons of advance ticket sales the Yankees would choose not to let that particular cat out of the bag until the following spring.

In later years, great players would be given farewell tours. Their retirement announced in advance, they would be saluted, presented with gifts, fondly recalled as worthy opponents as they made their last circuit around the league. Kaline would be afforded that kind of hail and farewell in seven more years. But it was unknown in 1968.

Mantle had been the very symbol of the Yankees teams that destroyed so many Detroit hopes during the '50s and '60s. He was the biggest attraction on the best team in baseball. Worshipped in New York, he was the one whom people in other cities came out to cheer, to boo, to admire, and to detest. He was now only a shadow of the great athlete who had flashed across the outfield grass in those years, the slugger who put the phrase "tape measure home run" into the language. He limped, his bat was slow. He was not yet thirty-seven but seemed far older.

But as he walked to the plate in Detroit for the last time, the small crowd in Tiger Stadium spontaneously decided to salute the old adversary. Rising to their feet, they cheered for him wildly. If it wasn't with quite the same emotion that had rung out two nights before for the pennant, it was still with a great deal of respect. The Tigers also got to their feet in the dugout and applauded. They were led by Kaline, who may have been the one other player in the league who could have compared with Mantle in the prime of their careers. When Mantle heard the ovation he stopped in his tracks. He said later he got chills.

He had just sixteen homers for the year. That was Mantle's lowest total since his rookie year, aside from the 1963 season, when he played in just sixty-five games. He also was tied with Jimmie Foxx with 534 career home runs, which was then the third highest in major league history. Only Babe Ruth and Willie Mays had hit more. But the way Mantle was swinging, it appeared unlikely that he could break the tie.

Mantle settled in, and what happened next has as many versions as the 50,000 people who claim to have been in the park that day. On a one-strike count, McLain made a waist-high motion across his body, indicating that that's where the next pitch would be. Everyone saw it, but Mantle didn't quite believe it. He swung early on the perfect fastball and hit it foul down the first baseline. Mantle stepped out and stared out at McLain, then motioned subtly for him to put the ball in the same place. Denny, with perfect control, obliged, and Mantle deposited it in the right-field upper deck.

As he trotted around the bases for the last time in Detroit, the crowd again rose to cheer for him. The home run ball had found its way back to the Detroit dugout, and Kaline held it up to Mantle, then rolled it across the diamond to the Yankees dugout.

Mantle, eventually, did hit another home run before the season ended and finished his career with 536. But no one who saw number 535 will ever forget it, courtesy of that consummate showman, that master of mirth, Dennis Dale McLain.

Strangely enough, with Detroit leading 6–2 the Yankees put two runners on in the ninth with Jake Gibbs coming to bat. If Gibbs had reached base, that would have brought Mantle to bat again, this time as the tying run. McLain, however, disposed of Gibbs on a fly ball, and that scenario, so rich in ironic possibilities, never developed.

But a far greater irony was taking shape for the Tigers. With the team heading to the World Series, there was no room in the lineup for one of the greatest players in the club's history. Al Kaline had become the odd man out.

CHAPTER 24

Six

Oakland Hills is known in Detroit as the country club for those who take golf seriously. The top executives, the ones who drive the automotive industry, belong to Bloomfield Hills Country Club, which is a trifle more chichi. It is at Oakland Hills, however, that major national tournaments are held. Its Men's Grille is one of the city's genuine power centers. Major players gather there daily, attacking the business world in the same way they go after the club's famed South Course.

This is Al Kaline's turf. This is where he hangs out when he isn't on the road as a broadcaster with the Tigers television crew. Schmoozing with pals, trying to shave a stroke off his game, spending the long summer afternoons.

To hang at the Men's Grille at Oakland Hills is a mark of success, a badge of belonging to a small circle of achievers. But even here, in the select company of life's lucky winners, Kaline is somehow set apart.

"Just this week, a middle-aged man, nicely dressed, suit and tie, obviously successful, came over to our table here," Kaline says.

"He said he just always wanted to meet me and shake my hand. That always puzzles me. I'm not one who likes to live in the past. I haven't played ball in more than twenty years, and in my mind that all happened a long time ago. I'm very serious about being a broadcaster, and today my mind is set on making sure I have something worthwhile to say. Not that I'm disconnected from what I was, but for me it's all part of the past.

"I know that I must symbolize something to people. But I really don't understand what it is."

That "it" is one of the reasons, however, that Kaline usually goes to the club when he eats out. He cannot get through a meal in peace at a restaurant. Not in Detroit.

James Michener once wrote of an incident he observed during the 1960 presidential campaign. A group of celebrities had been brought into Pennsylvania to help pump up the crowds. Among them was Stan Musial. The voters edged right up to the show business and literary personalities in easy familiarity. But they hung back from Musial, as if in awe. He was, after all, the Man. Just as Kaline was Six.

Some of the other Tigers called him Big Al, in reference to his status more than to his physical size. To others, he was the Line. A few of the irreverent referred to him as the Salary Cap, the top paycheck from which all the others on the team were ratcheted down. But most often they gave him the ultimate accolade one ballplayer can give another. They called him simply by the number on his uniform: Six.

And yet there remains, even now, a certain ambivalence toward Kaline among the men who were his teammates. Even in middle age, some of them might feel that he was not everything he might have been, that somehow he left them short-changed.

He truly was, in Colavito's words, "a little tin god" in the Detroit organization. His relationship with Campbell was different than that of any of the other players. It was more a meeting of peers than a boss telling his employee how things were going to be. He was the soul of the franchise, and Campbell recognized that. Kaline, despite (or maybe because of) his upbringing in a working-class Baltimore home, shared Campbell's conservative outlook when it came to finances. He understood the larger picture. They spoke the same language.

Kaline was also a private man, one who remained well within himself. Friendly but always holding back some private corner. He was never cut out to be a leader of men. He had no speeches to make when the clubhouse doors were closed, no inspirational messages to impart. He led by the way he played. Even in the major leagues, players are conscious that there are a few who are involved in a different game, whose skill level is unattainable to most others. Kaline was one of these. "You almost have to watch him play every day to appreciate what he does," said Johnny Podres after coming to the Tigers from the National League. "You hear about him, sure, but you really can't understand until you see him. He just never makes a mistake."

But the admiration was not universal. Some of the younger players resented him. They felt he deliberately set himself apart from the rest of them, that he was aloof, that his role as starter was not above question. They whispered that he would not play through injuries. Even now, one of the Tigers insists that on the last weekend of 1967, with the pennant on the line, Kaline sat out two of the final four games with California. In fact, Kaline started all four and played every inning, starting off one of the last rallies of the futile final game with a perfectly conceived bunt single. But the perception, some of it based on petty jealousy, remains.

After the 1966 season, the Dodgers made a fairly serious attempt at getting Kaline, packaging several of their younger prospects in an offer made at the winter meetings. Campbell wouldn't even consider it, because Kaline was as fixed as any superstar in any sport ever had been in the life of Detroit. Right out of high school to the Tigers without spending a day in the minors. Batting champion before his twenty-first birthday. A defensive range so wide that the Tigers had to remove several rows of box seats from the deepest part of the right-field corner to protect him from injury. Master of the big play. All that was missing, all that kept him from the level of Gordie Howe, Bobby Layne, Charlie Gehringer, and the other icons of the city's athletic past, was a championship.

Although Kaline may not like to dwell on the past, there are some moments that don't fade away. His ninth-inning catch of Mickey Mantle's drive at Yankee Stadium, leaping into the right-field seats to take away a game-winning home run, is one of the best.

"The New York radio crew couldn't believe I caught the ball," he says. "They went off the air saying the Yankees had won the game. The clubhouse man was listening and expected us to come off the field all down. Instead, he saw us running down the tunnel, yelling like crazy, and he didn't know what the heck was going on. Another time I drove in all the runs for Detroit in a game and Mickey did the same for the Yankees. The headline in one of the New York papers read: 'Kaline 3, Mantle 2.'

"I always enjoyed competing against Mickey. But, of course, it was never really me against him. Baseball is a game of individuals but within the team framework. One or two players can't make that much of a difference. You can't have a Michael Jordan come in and just turn an entire team around. That's what made '68 such a unique experience. For once, everything clicked as a team.

"You know, baseball is a game that you measure in failure. You fail seven times in ten at-bats, and you're a great player. Where else in life can you fail that often and be a success? I played twenty-two years in Detroit and won only once. That means there were a lot of seasons we came up empty.

"We were just so confident that year. I never played on a team that went out every day knowing that they were going to win. I can't tell you why that was. Maybe it was the right mix of veterans and younger guys. Maybe it was a holdover from the previous season when we lost a pennant we all know we should have won. But it was great to be a part of. Although, of course, it was a little frustrating for me, not playing all the time. I finally had to face the fact that if the team was stronger by my not being there, that's just how it was."

No one really understood what it was like, though. How it must have felt to go from being Six to becoming an occasional starter, scrambling for his at-bats like a utility man. He won an August game with a looping single, not quite the crisp liner that was a Kaline hallmark. Afterward, a writer lightly inquired, "What kind of a hit do you call that?" Kaline bristled in anger. "What kind of question do you call that?" he responded and stalked away. It hurt way too much to laugh.

"I understood the kind of pressure Mayo was under," he says. "It seemed that every day in September there was some kind of story speculating on what would happen to me during the series. So after we clinched the pennant, I went into Mayo's office and told him: 'Look, don't feel that you've got to play me. I understand the situation. It wouldn't be right to sit one of the kids, because they're the ones who won it for you.' Mayo just looked over and smiled and thanked me. Then he said to start working out at third base. That floored me. I'd played one or two games there for a few innings. But never consistently. So I took some infield there, and then a few days later Mayo called in me with a few of the other veterans—Cash, Mathews, Freehan. He asked us what we thought about moving Mickey Stanley to shortstop. That's the first any of us guessed what he'd been thinking.

"I never really felt any added pressure, knowing that the move had been made to get me in. I figured it was done to make us a stronger team, not as any favor to me. If I just stayed under control and played my game, we'd be fine."

In 1968, Kaline's Hall of Fame credentials were still regarded as debatable. He was seven hundred hits shy of 3,000, had not yet had the chance to perform on the national stage. As it turned out, he played long enough to reach 3,000 and breezed into Cooperstown in his first year of eligibility. But it was the World Series that really removed all doubts. It gave the entire country the chance to watch how Six played ball.

It is late afternoon, long past the lunch hour, and the Men's

Grill is almost empty. One group sits in the far corner, engaged in a game of cards. They look much older than Kaline. Even in his sixties, it wouldn't seem incongruous to see him in uniform. The face is a bit fuller, the hair a little grayer. But time has been good to him.

Besides his physical skills, Kaline also had an exceptionally fast mind. He was always aware of situations and personnel, always one step ahead of the next guy. In a game against Minnesota, Tony Oliva cranked one into the upper deck, deep in right center. But Kaline gave it the full fake, racing back to the wall as if he had a chance. He knew that Cesar Tovar, who was on first, was an aggressive baserunner and might tag up on the chance that Kaline would catch the ball and not be in position to throw. Sure enough, Tovar tagged, and Oliva, already into his home run trot, passed him at first base. Oliva was called out, and although Tovar was waved around to score, Kaline had taken a certain run away from the Twins. No one could recall ever seeing a play like it.

So with that kind of mental agility why did he never become a manager?

"They never asked me," he says. "Jim Campbell once mentioned that I'd have to go down to the minors for several years, and that didn't have much appeal to me. I never saw the sense in it. But it got to the point where I figured that if I had to ask, it wouldn't have been worth it. And besides, if I had asked and they didn't want to do it, how were they going to tell me no? It would have been too embarrassing for everyone.

"But I like to observe. I've always studied people. That's the only way to learn. After a while, you get to see tendencies, and that tells you a lot about a person. I try to bring some of that into the booth as a broadcaster. I don't run people down, but I try to give my opinion honestly. I've reached the point where I'm pretty comfortable with it."

In his early years as a broadcaster, Kaline was criticized for grammatical errors and mangled syntax. It stung him deeply. His formal education had ended with high school, but he is an avid

reader, deeply interested in political affairs. He worked to polish
his performance on the air with the same ethic he had brought
to baseball.

"It's funny," he says, "but, you know, Tiger Stadium is the only
place I've ever worked. I've been there since 1953, as a player
and a broadcaster. There was never any other place I got a paycheck from. So I have this feeling that I'll go on working until
the Tigers move to a new ballpark. That feels right to me.

"Come to think of it, maybe there's another reason I never
managed. I know that when I was growing up, ballplayers were
bigger than life. You really looked up to them. That's not true
anymore. You watch some of these guys, and there doesn't seem
to be any genuine love for the game or for their team or the city
they play in. You want to ask them what they have to be unhap-
py about. Maybe I'd find that too hard to deal with."

Maybe he had just answered his own question, too. Maybe
that's why successful middle-aged men still approach him with
the heart of the children they used to be, the same way a generation of New Yorkers felt about Mantle and mourned his death
as a terrible personal loss. Six is part of a Detroit generation's
land of lost content. Members of that generation know they can
never return. But seeing Six reassures them that something of
value remains.

CHAPTER 25

The Big Finish

After a pennant is clinched, a ball club usually gets to relax and take a short mental vacation before entering the pressure of the postseason. The remaining games are almost like exhibitions, with major stars rested, rookies inspected, and secondary pitchers given a chance to show what they can do. Detroit had wrapped it up with ten games still to go, which normally would have been an unusually long respite. But the last few games of the 1968 season would be anything but normal. The ball club began an experiment that would turn into one of the most audacious gambles in baseball history. For the final six games of the season, Mickey Stanley would start at shortstop. Mayo and his coaches would then determine whether or not Stanley could play there during the series.

It is hard now to recapture just how incredible this move was. With Kaline's performance in the series a part of the historical record, it now seems as if it was the only natural move to make. But there was nothing in the history of Mayo as a manager, or the

Tigers as an organization, that would have indicated a willingness to make a move quite so bold.

Detroit was one of the most conservative franchises in a game that resisted change with teeth firmly clenched and both heels dug in. Every so often, someone inside baseball would suggest that the sport consider changing with the times. But no one really thought he meant it. Baseball's response to the hippie-dippie world of 1968, an America going through one of the greatest cultural upheavals in its history, was to ignore it and hope it all went away. Facial hair was still forbidden on the Tigers and most other teams. Hair length was regulated. Ties and jackets were mandatory on planes and in hotel lobbies on the road. In the birthplace of Motown, the sound that was transforming the recording industry, the stadium organist was instructed to play only bouncy tunes from the '20s and polkas. It sounded like a Rotarian picnic. Another sixteen years and a public outcry would be required before the ball club would permit a tape of Detroit's unofficial summertime anthem, Martha and the Vandellas singing "Dancing in the Streets," with its joyful shout of "Can't forget the Motor City," to be played at Tiger Stadium.

The tone was set by general manager and executive vice president Jim Campbell. He was a man with the heart of an outfielder but the soul of an accountant. Campbell had played baseball at Ohio State University, graduated as a business major, and made a commitment to spend a life in baseball. It became his entire life. His marriage collapsed because he could not tear himself away from the ballpark. There was always another scouting report to read, another financial statement from the minors, another old story to tell in the hospitality room. He worked backbreaking hours, in his office by 9:00 A.M. and at the park one hour beyond the last out of a night game. He expected the rest of his staff to be there, too. When the team went on the road he wanted telephone reports from those traveling with the ball club first thing in the morning.

He was nothing if not methodical. He lived frugally himself, handling money as if it might explode in his face. Even thirty years later, players recount their contract battles with him like war stories, a war on which they, inevitably, were on the losing side. Those who went on to successful business careers understand now what Campbell was trying to do. Even so, most of them still feel they had to fight for every dollar and might have been more handsomely compensated for their achievements by another, more generous organization.

It is still legendary among the Tigers how Kaline turned down a $100,000 contract because he didn't feel that he had earned it. To contemporary fans, fed up with the unceasing whining and demands of millionaire players, it sounds like the selfless gesture of a noble spirit. But the rest of the Tigers groaned. Campbell would turn the anecdote upon them repeatedly with the question: "Do you think you're a better player than Kaline?"

But Campbell loved the game and everything about it. He understood his limitations as a judge of baseball talent and surrounded himself with knowledgeable former players. Campbell was especially devoted to George Kell and Rick Ferrell and made it a personal mission to see that both of them were elected to Cooperstown. When he traveled, he'd seek out the baseball hangouts, the restaurants run by former players. Those of Al Lopez in Tampa, Stan Musial in St. Louis, Tommy Henrich in Columbus, Ohio. He almost felt a responsibility to patronize these places. It was standing up for baseball. Campbell hated outlandish promotions, too. Occasionally he would grudgingly schedule a giveaway day or, even more rarely, a fireworks display. But he thought of all such marketing tools as crass gimmicks. He felt that the game was good enough to sell on its own merits. Nothing more was needed.

Campbell himself reflected the personality of the team's owner, Kalamazoo broadcasting executive John Fetzer. With his inside knowledge of the television industry, Fetzer would structure the first big-money network television package for the game, bringing in money beyond most of the owners' wildest dreams of avarice. The fact that this bonanza ultimately would lead to the spiraling salaries of free agency is yet another proof of the law of unintended consequences. Fetzer himself was stolid, Midwestern, conservative. After the death of his wife, he would dabble in spiritualism and attempt to make contact with the dead. But in the '60s he was the very model of old-fashioned values, a hands-off owner who lived 150 miles away and rarely showed up in the clubhouse. He was content to let Campbell run the club as he saw fit.

Mayo had been the perfect managerial choice for this organization. Whatever else he may have been, he was above all safe and predictable. Many Detroit observers had urged Campbell to pick a manager like Billy Martin, someone to rock the boat and shake things up, someone with new ideas. But new ideas were the last thing the Tigers wanted. Campbell, eventually, did hire Martin. Although Martin won a division title in 1972 the experience was a near-disaster for the organization and frequently reduced Campbell to a sputtering wreck.

Mayo was hardly a daring tactician. As far as he was concerned, the game pretty much ran itself. He managed by the book, inserting the right player in the game to do what he was supposed to do. If you had the better talent, things would turn out fine. If you didn't . . . oh, well. Taking a gifted centerfielder and turning him into a shortstop in one week did not quite fall within that style of managing.

Still, there was one value that was predominant in this organization. That was loyalty. If you produced and kept your mouth shut, you were taken care of. With all that Kaline had meant to the Detroit organization, it would have been unthinkable for Campbell to take away his place in the series. It would have been a denial of who Campbell was and how he defined his ball club. Mayo understood that. It made what he did inevitable.

The Tigers took enormous pride in being a self-made winner. Of all the starters, only Cash and Wilson had played in the majors for other teams. Campbell did not enjoy making trades, taking an accountant's very sensible view that if you wanted something of value you also had to give up something of value. He hated when that happened. Cash had been a steal, a lucky guess, with only a minor league infielder forfeited. Wilson had been obtained straight up for Don Demeter, a centerfielder made expendable by the emergence of young players from the farm system. (Oddly enough, both Cash and Wilson had been obtained for players named Demeter. In Cash's case, it was Steve Demeter. The two Demeters are the only two players of that name ever to appear in the majors.)

Lasher had pitched briefly w[...] in several years with the Dodg[...] and McMahon traveled widely in ot[...] out of the Pittsburgh chain. Othe[...] me through the Detroit system.

If the team had a major flaw[...] ers finished dead last in the majors [...] stolen bases with twenty-six, or fewer than half as many as Lou Brock swiped all by himself. The strategic revolution that the Dodgers and Maury Wills had wrought in the early '60s, bringing back the steal as a major offensive weapon, was already having an impact on the game. As teams started moving out of the pre-World War I bandboxes and into the larger, all-purpose stadiums, with formidably deep power alleys, the steal would become even more important. But that was still a few years away, and Tiger Stadium was still regarded as the best hitter's park in the game. Ever since the introduction of the live ball changed the game in 1920, this was a franchise based on power hitting. Only one pitcher in Detroit history, Hal Newhouser, would be voted into the Hall of Fame. (Jim Bunning went in as a member of the Phillies.) Winning in that ballpark was extraordinarily difficult, which made McLain's achievement that much more remarkable. The Tigers were always a team that eschewed the steal, preferring to wait for the long ball and score in clusters. In the 1970s, that would put them at a tremendous disadvantage as their farm system kept sending up the same kind of players. But for now that strategy was more than adequate.

The Tigers did have some runners in Stanley, Northrup, and McAuliffe. But their speed served mostly as a defensive advantage.

This was the best fielding team in the majors by a big margin. It made only 105 errors—with the runner-up committing 119. Detroit did not give away ball games. This again was mandated by the sort of park in which it played. Poor fielding teams could not survive Tiger Stadium because its dimensions did not forgive mistakes.

This ball club had been crafted deliberately by Campbell and his advisors. To Campbell it all was a gigantic game of chess. He understood the rules thoroughly and had mastered the endgame. When it all began to change with free agency in the late '70s, Campbell became almost disspirited. The rules were different. In his mind, it had degenerated into a brainless contest to spend the most money. There was no challenge. Moreover, the movement of players destroyed the sense of continuity and the loyalty that he valued so highly. He increasingly withdrew from the daily running of the team and concentrated on the business aspects. It was as if he understood that the game he knew had passed.

But in 1968 Campbell had put all the pieces into place. On September 28, he received his reward. On this next-to-last home game of the season, the Tigers went over the two million mark in attendance. A mark thought to be unattainable in Detroit, with its unpredictable weather and obstructed-view seats and nervous populace, had been exceeded. The season had been a success in the ledgers as well as on the field. Now the honest accountant was preparing to risk it all with a roll of the dice at shortstop.

CHAPTER 26

On Dangerous Ground

"**I**'m a workaholic," he confesses cheerfully. It's only 8:00 A.M., but Mickey Stanley has already cleared off a day's work from his desk in his little office near Brighton, at the very edge of suburban Detroit's outward growth. Now he will get down to the real labor at hand, running a backhoe to clear a property he is developing a few miles away.

"I've got two new subdivisions starting up just north of here, and we're running behind," he says. "I've never minded getting my hands a little dirty.

"It started when I got out of baseball, I guess. I got nervous. I had $15,000 in the bank and a family to support. I had my fun, and now it was time to get serious about life. I've been pretty much out of the public eye ever since. I see some of the other guys turning up on television or radio. Not me. Maybe I overdo it a little on work. But I can't turn off the machine."

With his clean-cut, blond good looks, Stanley among the

Tigers always looked a bit like Jack Armstrong thrown in with a gang of pirates. He was the best athlete on the team, in a sport where the best athletes do not always win. He loved everything about being a ballplayer. The conditioning, the warm-ups that others found onerous, to Stanley were a joy. Running sprints, catching fungoes, taking infield—he loved it all. That, eventually, proved the Tigers' salvation and his undoing.

"The shortstop thing just hit me right out of the blue, though," he says. "I didn't have any inkling that this was going to happen. It must have been Cash. He always saw me fielding grounders out there during infield drill. But I was fooling around. I loved being on the field. I was just a big kid. I lived to play ball. Sure, Mayo had played me there a few times before. But to me it was like practice, to fill in in an emergency or something. But I think that Cash put a bug in his ear.

"We all knew something had to give about getting Kaline in the lineup. We'd heard maybe third base. The Cards had already announced that they would throw nothing but right-handers at us, so platooning him at first wasn't going to work. We were in Baltimore on the last Monday of the season and Mayo called me up to his room at the hotel. He told me that he was going to play me the last six games at shortstop and if it worked out that I would start there in the series.

"I wasn't afraid to do it. In fact, it was kind of flattering. If the ball club had that much confidence in me, it must have meant something good. And if I screwed up in the last six games, who cared? I decided to just see what happened. So I go out there that night against the Orioles, and they don't like us much anyhow. McLain walks Don Buford, the leadoff man. The next guy hits one down to Cash, and he throws to me for the force. And Buford just comes in and knocks me right on my ass. 'Hmm,' I told myself, 'this is going to be interesting.'

"I throw the ball away for an error. My first play in the big experiment, and already I have an error. This was not going so well."

Stanley muffed a grounder later in the same game. But over the last five games, his fielding was flawless. Mayo, however, refused to give a definite answer. His remarks to the press after the last game of the season were couched in such noncommittal terms that one of the Detroit papers came out the next day with a story that Stanley definitely would be the series shortstop—and the other paper declared that he would not.

"I knew it was going to happen," says Stanley. "That's when it started to get to me. I was so comfortable in center field. I knew in my mind that when I was out there nothing was going to hit the green. I was familiar with every situation. It all clicked in my mind. Gold Glove. I played all year out there and never made an error. That tied a record. To be taken out of that situation and put at shortstop. It was like landing in alien territory."

Strangely enough, most of the Tigers had complete confidence in Stanley. They felt about him much as the contemporary Detroit Lions felt about their star cornerback, future Hall of Famer Lem Barney. The nickname for Barney was The Supernatural because he could do anything on a football field. Similarly, Stanley's teammates felt that he could play anywhere on the diamond.

He had come out of Grand Rapids, one of the top high school athletes in the city's history, and signed a baseball contract at the age of eighteen. But whereas defense came easily to him, hitting was a struggle. He advanced through the Tigers system, one rung at a time, taking a year longer to get to the big club than most of the others in his class. This season had been a breakthrough year for him as a hitter, and he was elevated to the number-two slot in the lineup. But it was on defense, with his uncanny ability to get a jump on a ball, that he shone. Whereas other center fielders excelled on sheer speed, Stanley seemed to be operating on clair-voyance, getting to many balls simply on anticipation.

"I think it was Frank Carswell, the manager at Knoxville, at Double A, who shook me up," he says. "They sent me back down there for a second year after I couldn't hit at Triple A. Frank took me aside when I got there and told me: 'Look, either you start taking advantage of your abilities, Stanley, or you're not going to make enough money to buy a warm-up jacket for a pissant.' I hit .300 for him that year, and after that it started coming to me.

"But when I walked on the field for that first series game in St. Louis, it all kind of hit me. Norm Cash told me that I was so tight they couldn't have pulled a pin out of my ass with a tractor. It was horrible. I might have never let on what I was going through at the time, but, believe me, it was a terrible experience. I couldn't sleep at all. I always felt that I got cheated out of my series. It was no fun for me at all.

"Brock [...] Cardinals, and he was so damn sma[...] ng to inside-out the ball, going out o[...] e did it, and I threw him out. At leas[...] after that. I got the jitterbugs out. [...] ver really left me. It was always pretty [...] e spikes or anything like that, and I kne[...] to be on the plays. I just understood that Mayo had really stuck his neck out a mile and it was up to me that he didn't get it chopped off.

"I ended up making two errors. I kicked away a ball that Julian Javier hit in the hole. And I backhanded one ball, and my throw pulled McAuliffe off the bag on the force. So two bad plays and no runs scored on either one. That was pretty good, huh?

"Of course, what happened afterwards wasn't so good. Mayo told me to start working out at short the next spring. I was feeling pretty cocky, and I started cutting loose on my throws without really getting ready. I hurt my arm, and I never really got it back to full strength for the rest of my career. I played a bunch of games there in 1969, but then we got Eddie Brinkman two years later, and there was no need for anyone else to play shortstop.

"The thing that stays in my mind was how great Ray Oyler took it all. He was just a first-class guy. We were pretty good friends, and I knew this just had to be killing him. To get into the series and then have some guy moved entirely out of position to take your place. But he acted like there was no problem. He'd take me out there during workouts and tried to give me a crash course in shortstop. He was such a great competitor. He played hurt, he played hungover. He never complained. We all loved that guy.

"But that's how it was with that team. We all were confident in each other, we trusted each other's abilities. Everyone contributed.

"After I left baseball, I did pretty well in the business world. I've tried to take care of my family and be a good Christian. Maybe baseball left me a little bit naive. But I know that there's always somebody out here trying to screw you. A lot of us came off that team and did very well in life. We had enough savvy to succeed in more than baseball. And I know to this day that I'd trust every one of them. No question in my mind. That's the kind of people they were."

CHAPTER 27

Demolition Derby

The last six games of the regular season may have been a hectic experience for Mickey Stanley. But they were a bit of a lull in the life of Denny McLain.

After the high drama of the thirtieth win and the pennant clincher and the Mantle home run, Denny needed a little something to keep his interest up. So upon being asked his view of the upcoming World Series, he responded: "I'm sick of hearing about what a great team the Cardinals are. I don't want to just beat them; I want to demolish them."

Oh, my.

In the trash-talking, in-your-face '90s, this sort of hype has become commonplace. Even four months later, Joe Namath would cause whole forests of newsprint to be felled to convey the news that he "guaranteed" a Super Bowl for the New York Jets over the heavily favored Baltimore Colts. But McLain beat him to it, and with a far more pronounced sneer on his lips.

The Cardinals were decided favorites going into this series, although certainly not by the overwhelming margin that the

Colts would be. The Tigers were seen as fairly formidable opponents by the oddsmakers. But for the Cards, this was their third series in five years, and they were loaded with money players.

The core of this Cardinals team had upended the Yankees in 1964 and then come back to defeat Boston in 1967. There had been a fairly extensive makeover of the infield between the two championships. Only second baseman Julian Javier remained at the same position. But Lou Brock and Curt Flood were back in the outfield, and Mike Shannon had moved from right field to third base. Tim McCarver was the catcher on both teams. Although the pitching staff had been overhauled almost entirely, Bob Gibson was the rock on which it was built.

McLain's season had been historic. But Gibson's stats read like something out of the dead-ball era. His 1.12 ERA had not been matched in more than half a century. Thirteen of his twenty-two wins had been shutouts. He finished all but six of his starts. These numbers didn't have the immediate grab of thirty wins. But to those with a sense of history and a knowledge of how the game had evolved, they were staggering. They had the texture of Walter Johnson in his prime.

Moreover, Gibson had already proven that he could do it on the field as well as in the scorebook. He had won five series games in a row, beating the Yankees twice and then polishing off the Red Sox three times. In those five games, he had struck out forty-eight men and pitched with the efficiency of a scythe, ruthlessly cutting down everything in his path.

Gibson was anger turned to grace. A man filled with the fury of racial discrimination, he had managed to channel it more artfully than any player since Jackie Robinson. A complete athlete, he fought the opposition with his arm, his legs, his bat; and you got the idea that if those didn't work he'd take on the opposition with his fingernails. The Tigers thought they knew a little something about him from the times they had faced him in Florida exhibitions. As it turned out, they didn't know a thing. They would now encounter a different Gibson, one prepared for mortal combat.

"I couldn't ignore what Denny said," Gibson now recalls. "I'm sure he regretted it as soon as it left his mouth. I had nothing against him personally. In fact, I kind of admired the way he marketed himself. He understood where the bottom line was in this game. I just didn't think any pitcher could beat me in a World Series. I sure as hell didn't think Denny McLain could do it.

"I'm pretty sure I knew more about him than he did about me. I thought he was as much a showman as he was a competitor. That thing about giving up the home run to Mantle. Disgraceful. I would have dropped my pants on the mound before deferring to an opposing player that way. You know what I would have done to show my respect for Mantle? I would have reached back for something extra and tried to blow him away."

Much has been made of the fact that on the days that Gibson pitched the Cardinals fielded a team with a majority of blacks and Hispanics in the lineup. There was Brock, Flood, Javier, and first baseman Orlando Cepeda. Writer David Halberstam contrasted them to their 1964 series opponents, the Yankees, and concluded that the Cards, at the peak of the civil rights era, presented a vision of an integrated America. Claiming that as a unique niche for this team, however, is a bit of a stretch. The championship Dodgers ballclub of 1955 could also field five minority starters—Robinson, Jim Gilliam, Roy Campanella, Sandy Amoros, and Don Newcombe. The 1962 San Francisco Giants, who lost the series to the Yankees, would often present a lineup with six minority members.

If the Cards played a different style of game than the Tigers, that had more to do with the exigencies of their home stadium than with any ethnic or racial background. St. Louis had been one of the first cities to build the all-purpose, circular, cookie-cutter stadium. Although "all-purpose" was the acceptable euphemism, these facilities were usually built to favor a football configuration. Within a generation, they would be regarded as hopelessly obsolete, unsatisfactory for either sport, candidates for the wrecking ball. Baseball, especially, suffered, with seats too far from the field, power alleys too long, artificial surfaces that distorted the speed of the ball. When new ballparks were built in the 1990s they were more likely to borrow features from struc- tures such as Tiger Stadium, ballparks with a sense of place and historic ambience to them. Such places proved wildly popular in many cities, especially Cleveland, Baltimore, Denver, and Arlington, Texas, where attendance records were shattered. But in 1968, the circular park was thought to be the shape of things to come, and the Cards were the team of the era.

They came at opponents with overwhelming speed and pitch- ing. Cepeda and Shannon were the only consistent power threats in the lineup, and they hit just seventeen and sixteen homers, respectively. Except for Shannon, in fact, everyone in their line- up had dropped off significantly in offense from the previous year. Even Brock, a holy terror in the 1967 series, had finished the sea- son at just .279, with a mere six homers. Roger Maris, who had slammed his sixty-one homers only seven years before, was at the end of the road. He was a smarter hitter but one whose extra-base threat was only a memory. Maris hit just five homers all season.

Behind Gibson, there was nineteen-game winner Nellie Briles and Ray Washburn, who had won fourteen. These were manager Red Schoendienst's choices to start the other series games. Detroit's scouts had reported that neither one would present much of a problem to the Tigers' power hitters. Schoendienst decided to bypass future Hall of Famer Steve Carlton in his series rotation, using him in long relief. Carlton had been the least of the team's four starters, with a 13–11 record. Moreover, Detroit had pounded lefties at a .655 pace during the season. Carlton was just twenty-three and not yet the pitcher who would become the best in the National League through the '70s. Still, he had start- ed in the 1967 series, and the Tigers respected his arm far more than they did that of Washburn or Briles. They thought Schoendienst was doing them a favor.

So there would be just one-left handed starter for either side in this series. That would be Lolich. He had come on so late and so fast, and was so overshadowed by McLain, that the St. Louis book on him was inconclusive. "Stay close, and you'll beat him," was the phrase they used, but the same thing could have been said about any number of pitchers in the majors. Lolich was the X factor in the series. St. Louis, however, didn't think they would have to get much beyond G in the alphabet. With Gibson starting three times, the Cards were confident that they had the edge in pitching.

This was a very confident team about most things. From the multicolored ball they used in infield practice (a quirk the Tigers had copied) to the nickname "El Birdos" that they had hung on themselves, it was a club that had its own strong identity. The Cards understood precisely what it took to win. Their final pennant margin of nine games was a bit smaller than Detroit's. But they had removed all doubt from the race even earlier than the Tigers and coasted in from mid-August on. The previous year they had won by 10½. The Cards knew they were very good and played that way.

So they were amused rather than seriously angered by McLain's little diatribe. But they hung it in their locker room at Busch Stadium. Gibson, who was angry most of the time anyhow, knew he would get the starting assignment against McLain. He did not need the diatribe to motivate him.

The two franchises had met once before in a series, in 1934. Oddly enough, those games involved the last pitcher to have won thirty games, Dizzy Dean. He had combined with his brother, Paul, to win forty-nine for the Cards that year. Before the series, he had flat out proclaimed that "me 'n' Paul" would win the four games needed to beat the Tigers. As it turned out, he was right on the money. He didn't say anything about demolition. But as he himself pointed out on another occasion, "If you can do it, it ain't braggin'."

It remained to be seen whether McLain could do it or not.

CHAPTER 28

Duel in the Sun

It was once axiomatic in American politics that no serious presidential campaigning was done until after the World Series. That would leave the candidates about a month to go after each other. In more innocent years, that was regarded as more than ample time. But both politics and baseball have changed. With two rounds of playoffs in effect, the series now doesn't end until the last few days of October. Under the old time frame, that would result in a presidential campaign of about a week and a half—which would probably suit most voters just fine.

But even by 1968, when the series still ended before the autumn leaves had fallen, things were different. The campaign was in full cry. Two days before the opener, Vice President Hubert Humphrey promised to stop all bombing operations in North Vietnam, reversing the policy of his boss, Lyndon B. Johnson. Even in Detroit and St. Louis, this was front page news. Humphrey was thought to have scored major points over his opponent, Richard M. Nixon, who was planning to announce the same policy shift.

The war raged on. By October of 1968, almost 30,000 American soldiers had been killed in Vietnam. This was slightly more than half of the total number who would eventually have their names inscribed on the memorial wall in Washington, D.C. Although sporadic antiwar demonstrations on college campuses and city streets brought the idea of the war home, its reality was quite far away.

In Detroit's previous series appearance, in 1945, World War II had been over for about a month. Yet the country was still on a wartime footing. Travel restrictions applied, and the series was allowed to move only once between Detroit and Chicago. The rosters of both teams had been denuded of most stars. Industry still had not shifted back into consumer production. The war affected every aspect of the life of every individual in the country. During the single autumn that the United States was involved in World War I, the regular season ended at Labor Day, and special dispensation had to be granted for the 1918 World Series to proceed. But fifty years later, the war in Asia barely touched baseball and the crowds who would pack Tiger and Busch Stadiums. Aside from the few players who left for two weeks of summer training with their National Guard units, as far as baseball was concerned the war didn't exist.

McLain against Gibson. That was what mattered.

Never in recent history had a series pitching matchup been so eagerly anticipated. It was built up like a heavyweight championship match—the cool, destructive Joe Louis against the brash, big-mouthed Muhammad Ali. The two pitchers were interviewed in a full-blown, presidential-sized press conference on the day before they would finally meet. Both spoke in soft, complimentary terms. No talk of demolition now. They emphasized that all this talk of McLain versus Gibson was getting a little wearisome. More attention should be paid to the matchups of the teams. But no one bothered. This was to be mano y mano, a personal duel in the sun in the middle of the arena.

This year of the pitcher could have ended no other way. The achievements of Gibson and McLain and a few others had given pitchers the sort of dominance that hadn't been seen since the dead-ball era in the major leagues. Since 1964, the first time this Cardinals team went to the series, batting averages had dropped eleven points in the National League and seventeen points in the American. Scoring was down by more than 1,000 runs in each league. Carl Yastrzemski's .301 mark for the American League batting title was the lowest in history.

The owners were convinced that this was "Bad for Baseball." Baseball people actually talked like that in 1968. Being described as Bad for Baseball carried a powerful sense of condemnation, as if your patriotism had been found wanting or a copy of Mao's *Little Red Book* turned up among your personal belongings. Among other things that were Bad for Baseball were an irreverent attitude, beards and mustaches, rock and soul music, and a lifting of the game's exemption from federal antitrust regulations. But as a direct result of this season, a lowered pitcher's mound, a narrowed strike zone, and the designated hitter rule were all adopted. A round of expansion in 1969 also diminished the quality of most pitching staffs. By the early '70s, the Year of the Pitcher was only a horrible memory to the owners. But in 1968 it was the heart of the story.

McLain's motto for this encounter seemed to be: "What? Me worry?" He told reporters that he would be more on edge for his opening in Las Vegas, scheduled for later in the month. He then astonished the crowd in the bar at the Sheraton-Jefferson Hotel the night before the game by sitting down at the organ in the wee hours and giving an impromptu concert.

The confrontation finally came on a gorgeous Yom Kippur afternoon.

If the Tigers hadn't fully understood before, by the end of the third inning they knew they were in deep trouble. Gibson was unhittable, in full command of his entire arsenal. At no time in the American League season had they faced a pitcher like this, someone who threw this hard with this much movement on the ball. He struck out seven of the first ten men he faced. At one point, he mowed down Kaline, Cash, Horton, Northrup, and

Freehan—the heart of the Tigers lineup—right in a row. It was a demoralizing display of power pitching.

"He never wastes a round," said Horton. "He came out throwing as hard to the number nine hitter as to the number three hitter, as hard in the ninth inning as he did in the first."

"He surprised us with the curve," said Cash. "I kept looking for the high, hard one, and he kept breaking off one hellacious curve after another."

"Luis Tiant throws just as hard," insisted Northrup.

For the most part, however, the Tigers look scared, as if the first game of the series against a pitcher of this caliber was just a bit more than they could handle. For Kaline, who struck out three times, it was the first series game he had ever seen in person.

"Someone wrote that I had taken a vow never to see a series game until I got to play in one," he says. "That's silly. I never went to a series game because usually I was just too tired when the season ended to go travel somewhere."

The Tigers denied that they were anything like shell-shocked after this game. But they did have that look. They knew that they would see Gibson twice more and have to beat him once somehow if they hoped to win. Cash, sizing up the attitude around him, tried to put a light turn on things. "Someone should have warned us that he changed clothes in a phone booth before he got to the park and took off the suit with the big S on it," he said.

Gibson obliterated the single-game strikeout record of fifteen, set by Sandy Koufax in 1963. As Koufax watched from the television booth, Gibson tied the record by getting Kaline in the ninth. Then he broke it with Cash and finished up with seventeen strikeouts by ending the game with Horton.

"Honestly, I wasn't aware of the record," says Gibson. "I didn't even hear the crowd cheering. McCarver came out to the mound with the ball after I got Cash, and I had no idea what he was doing there. I told him to just give me the goddamn baseball and get back to the plate so we can get this finished.

"They were chasing my slider all day like it was a fastball. But it was what they said in the papers the next day that really stopped me. In the National League we'd never praise an opposing player like that. You didn't give him that kind of lavish respect. Losers did that."

McLain, meanwhile, struggled with his control from the outset, in trouble throughout the early innings. He was working from behind in the count consistently. Finally, in the fourth, he walked Maris and McCarver, then gave up singles to Shannon and Javier. The Cards had a 3–0 lead, and everyone knew that would be plenty. St. Louis added one for good measure on a Brock home run and finished with an emphatic 4–0 win.

There was no doubt now about who was the top heavyweight in baseball. The winner and still champion was Gibson. The Tigers now had to show that they were capable of dimming the lesser lights of St. Louis.

The next day it would be Lolich against Briles. This was almost an anticlimax. After all the expectations of the opener, it was regarded as routine. Lolich had finished the year with just seventeen wins and he didn't play even a harmonica. But Maris had warned his Cardinals teammates that when Lolich had his slider working, he could be enormous trouble. Moreover, the Tigers were sure that once they got the Cardinals back in Detroit, they would have their way with them. That's where their big advantage in power would come into play. But they had to win one time in St. Louis. Then they could go home all even again.

CHAPTER 29

The Doughnut Man

When he was still playing baseball, Mickey Lolich got an offer to go into the food business in Detroit.

"Guy called me up when he saw my last name was Croatian," says Lolich. "He told me that he was Macedonian and figured that put us in about the same neighborhood. He wanted to set me up with a pizza outlet. But I couldn't see it. There didn't seem to be much of a chance for growth with pizza, so I turned him down. The guy was Mike Ilitch, and he made so much money selling pizzas that he bought the ball club. So how smart does that make me?"

The morning rush has ended at Mickey Lolich's Doughnut Shop. The proprietor, dressed in suspenders and a plaid flannel shirt, sips coffee at a work counter in the rear of his place in Lake Orion. It's about a forty-five-minute drive from Tiger Stadium but just down the road from the Palace of Auburn Hills, home of the Detroit Pistons. An excellent location. Lolich has more invested in the place than just his name in the front window.

He's hands-on, at work every morning at the ovens. And not only hands. He had something of a potbelly even as a player. "It's hereditary," he would explain. As a doughnut shop owner, this part of his anatomy has expanded exponentially, further proof of his intimate involvement in the workings of his business.

"I can hardly remember a thing about the rest of the 1968 season," he says. "I know they sent me out to the bull pen in August, and I won something like four games in a week. Since I only won seventeen games all year, that means I must have been pretty much horseshit the rest of the time. The series, sure. I remember every inning, almost every pitch. But, you know, the years go along, and the seasons start running together. I have to stop and ask myself: 'Now, wait a minute, was that in '68, or did it happen in '72, when we won the division?' I pitched in a lot of ball games. You remember the people, but the details of the games all kind of blur.

"I never even expected to pitch in the major leagues. Just signing a minor league contract to me was the greatest thing in my life. I never had a winning season until I got to the Tigers. Things never came easy for me. I was never that kind of guy. I was always blue collar, just going out and doing the best job I could. They had me pigeonholed in the system as another screwy left-hander, and that always irritated me. I'm not really a left-hander. I just throw that way because I got into a motorcycle accident when I was a kid and couldn't use my right arm for a while. So to keep playing ball, I had to learn how to throw left-handed. But they had me pegged because I went my own way. Screwy left-hander.

"Even when I first got to Detroit, I didn't buy a house where the rest of the guys did. I wanted something that was a little more rural, farther away from the city. It took me a little longer to get to the stadium, but that never bothered me. It gave me more time to think, just me and the motorcycle. It clears your mind."

When Lolich moved out to the town of Washington, it was remote, barely inside the metropolitan area's orbit. But three decades later, the city has grown out to him. His doughnut shop, which is not far from his home, is located in a community that was primarily a summer lakeside resort in 1968. Now traffic through Lake Orion is so heavy during rush hours that local police refer to it as the Snake, an endless line of cars twisting off to the far horizon. The doughnut shop has become something of a tourist attraction. Baseball fans from around the country are constantly pulling in to look over the memorabilia displayed there, munch a cruller, and hope for a look at the great man himself.

Lolich drifted through the Detroit farm system for three years, never quite making it at the AA level. When they promoted him to AAA, he was treated brutally. So the Tigers lent him to the team in Portland, his Oregon hometown, on the supposition that he was no great loss. It was while pitching there, in the summer of 1962, that he put it together.

"I think it was the left-field fence," he says. "It was so close in that park that you couldn't make a mistake. I concentrated more, and my control improved. One year later, I was in Detroit."

By 1964, he was an eighteen-game winner and regarded as the young star of the Tigers staff. Then he stalled again. Although he never won fewer than fourteen games in the next three years, he didn't move on to a higher level, either. And when McLain arrived, he found himself challenged for the pre-eminent position.

"I don't think there was ever any great secret about the way Denny and I felt about each other," says Lolich. "I didn't hate him, no. It didn't bother me that he had become the number one pitcher. I never admitted to myself that I was number two. But I didn't like the way he made his own rules and got away with it. I came up with the Detroit organization, and you were taught that there was a certain way you conducted yourself. It was fairly well regimented. I didn't mind that, and neither did the other guys— just as long as the same rules applied to everyone.

"Denny never wanted to go along with the program. He always seemed to be challenging management, flaunting it, seeing what he could get away with. I remember the time he landed his plane at a little airport, and because he was in a hurry he left it block-ing the fuel pumps. Nobody else could gas up. That was how he did things."

The antagonism reached the public eye during the 1969 All-Star Game break. McLain gave Lolich and his wife a ride to the game in Washington, D.C., aboard his Cessna. But when the game was delayed by rain, McLain had to return to Detroit early, he said, to keep an urgent dental appointment. He says that Lolich knew of the time constraints and knew that he would have to make other transportation arrangements. Lolich insists, however, that McLain never said a word about an early departure. The first he knew about it was after the game when he went looking for his plane ride home and found it had already flown away.

For his part, McLain liked Lolich even less.

"We didn't need a U.N. peacekeeping force between us," McLain said in his 1988 autobiography, *Strikeout*. "We just went our separate ways, did our separate things, and went through the motions of sociability. . . .

"Lolich had a great arm, but he also had a personality that rubbed people the wrong way, especially me. Lolich was the kind of guy who could say 'Good morning' and piss you off. What bothered me was his petty jealousy. He couldn't stand to see other guys succeed. It seemed to me that Mickey sometimes pulled against the Tigers—and especially the other pitchers. I think that he secretly wished the Tigers would lose every game but the ones he pitched."

But McLain would not have been in the running for Mr. Congeniality on this team, either. During the 1969 season, in fact, when the network Game of the Week awarded cash prizes to players of the game (a quaint notion now given the salaries of the '90s) McLain openly pulled against his hitters in one game so that he could win the award instead. His accusations against Lolich may be what psychiatrists refer to as projection.

Several of the Tigers mentioned an incident in which McLain

was found cheating at cards in one of the ongoing games among the players. One of the other players had to be pulled off him. But that was how McLain operated.

Lolich, on the other hand, found himself bogged down in a constant search for respect. One local dealer, for example, gave him the use of a new car for the 1968 season. It was a luxury model and carried the dealer's name modestly displayed on the side. When Lolich was taken out of the rotation and sent to the bull pen, the dealer demanded his car back.

"I think Mayo took out a lot of his frustrations on me," Lolich says. "He didn't dare touch Denny, not with the season he was having. So I became the whipping boy. It was all right. The only thing I ever asked from any manager is that if you had to take me out of a ball game, don't point to the bull pen before you got to the mound. I thought that was disrespectful.

"But as for the series, maybe it was the ideal situation. There was no pressure on me. I just went out and pitched. I'd been throwing the ball good from the middle of August on. I just remember feeling very confident, very relaxed. My wife, Joyce, was on the road with me, and she said before the games in St. Louis that I slept like a baby. Maybe I did grind my teeth a little, but I do that anyhow.

"What really bothered me is that my dad and my uncle came to St. Louis to see me pitch, and they couldn't get a flight back out to Detroit. So I was trying to talk Jim Campbell into letting them on the team plane. I remember walking out to the mound worried about that. Campbell finally gave the OK. How was he going to turn me down? To me that was one of the greatest rewards of the whole experience, giving my dad and my uncle the chance to share in it. To this day my uncle still talks about it whenever I see him.

"But the series changed everything for me. It wasn't only about finally getting recognition. It was like I turned over a new leaf in my mind. I knew I was a good pitcher. But I was more confident about being able to challenge the hitters. I went after everyone."

When McLain had gone for his thirtiethth a few weeks before, Lolich had attached a sign shaped like an arrow to his locker, at the entrance to the Detroit clubhouse. "To McLain's locker," it read. There was a touch of spite about it. But now Lolich was the man. The crowd stopped at his locker. He went out in game two of the series and shut down the Cards, 8–1, striking out nine hitters on the way. Not quite in Gibson's league, but a strong game, nonetheless. And to top it off, he hit the first, and what would be the only, home run of his career. It was no gimme, either. It came in the third, with the Tigers ahead only 1–0. So unaccustomed was Lolich to this sort of thing that he missed first base on his first pass around. He had to be yelled back to touch the bag by first base coach Wally Moses. A display in the doughnut shop exhibits a bat with a hitting area about the size of a tennis racket. "The bat Mickey used to hit his series homer," it reads.

It didn't seem that he could improve on that pitching and hitting performance. But he would—and quickly, too. In just a few more days he would become a national hero and the idol of Michigan.

"That part of it lasted a minute and a half," he says. "The Vegas appearances, getting the *Sport Magazine* award, all the rest. I've just been a working stiff the rest of my life. A little overweight. Not real good looking. Just respecting my job and trying my best. It was real nice, but that's really not who I am."

In 1984, when the Tigers got back to the series, Lolich reported that the seats given to him by the club were deep in the upper deck of the outfield. He parked in a downtown lot and rode the shuttle bus to the ballpark with the rest of the fans. Hardly anyone recognized him. Although he had harbored ambitions to be a sports broadcaster after retirement, he didn't get a call until the spring of 1996. Then a new Michigan minor league franchise, the Lansing Lugnuts, asked him to be the color man on a few of their local telecasts. Why not? From doughnuts to lugnuts isn't that big a jump.

We left the doughnut shop through a back door and walked

into the parking lot. A man, getting into a car with Florida plates, looked up, saw Lolich, and did a double take. He then walked over to him.

"You're Mickey, aren't you?" said the visitor. "I was hoping I'd get to see you. I just want to tell you how much I admired you and shake your hand."

Lolich obliged, and the man beamed.

"Today I'll tell my grandson that I got to shake hands with a hero."

There are times when the events of a week can last a whole life through.

CHAPTER 30

The Final Comeback

About ten minutes into game five of the series, a wise guy spread the word through the press box that the baseball writers' chartered flight back to St. Louis had been cancelled. The series was, to all appearances, over. The Cards were about to finish a sweep in Detroit and wrap it up in five.

This is a sportswriter's dream. Most of them secretly pray for a five-game series to avoid the trek back to the original city and three more days away from home. It's the trade's dirty little secret.

With Orlando Cepeda putting a Lolich delivery into the left-field seats for a three-run homer in the first, it certainly looked as if their prayers would be answered.

Even in the Detroit bull pen, players were tallying up their losses.

"I remember sitting next to Don McMahon," says Jon Warden, "and he was trying to calculate the loser's share of the series pool. Maybe he was just trying to cheer me up, but he said it was going to be pretty close to what he got for winning in 1957. It was a big difference for me, since I was making the minimum. Those few thousand dollars were huge. Guys put down payments on their houses with that difference."

Detroit had waited a long time for these games. A huge tiger face had been painted on the pavement at the main downtown intersection of Michigan Avenue and Washington Boulevard. A song called "Go Get 'em, Tigers" blared from every radio. The entire city had decked itself out in flags and bunting, and throughout the weekend an air of carnival had taken hold.

But now it was the third game in Tiger Stadium, and Detroit had been clubbed twice. Wilson couldn't get past the fifth inning in game three. Cepeda and McCarver clubbed three-run homers, and the Cards, behind Washburn, had retaken the series lead with a 7–3 win. Then on Sunday had come outright humiliation. Gibson again simply overwhelmed the Tigers. They were catching up to him, though. He struck out only ten this time, and Northrup did manage to get a home run in the 10–1 St. Louis romp. But Gibson also hit a homer, and Brock, who was feasting on the Tigers, drove in four runs.

Brock had stolen seven bases in just four games, tying his own record set the previous year. But it had taken him seven games to do it then. Freehan could not begin to contain him. Brock was stealing at will, making it look as if he were playing with children. To make it worse, Freehan also had gone hitless in thirteen times at bat.

"He's not just doing it to me. It's the whole team that's going through this," said Freehan. "I'm not embarrassed. I wish I were playing better, but at this point I don't think it's anything that I have control over."

Brock had further annoyed the Tigers by stealing his record seventh base as the Cardinals were nine runs ahead. It was a major breach of the game's etiquette and vexed Detroit deeply.

McLain, however, was more than vexed. He announced that he was done. Brock had drilled his second pitch of the game for a home run, and it had gone downhill from there. McLain was gone by the third inning, driven out by an unrelenting St. Louis attack. The thirty-one wins were forgotten now. The Cards had exposed him as a pretender. He told reporters after the game that even if the Tigers managed to extend the series, he could not start a third time. His shoulder was throbbing with pain. His season was over.

The game itself had turned farcical. It was started in a steady rain. But the Sunday series game always drew the biggest TV audience of the week, even going up against pro football. A postponement was out of the question. In 1968, all series games were still played in the daylight. Baseball harbored the quaint notion that it was important to showcase its biggest event to the widest audience, even including children. The first night game in the series was still three years away. By the end of the '80s, all games, even those on the weekends, were played at night and often did not end until midnight when all good little boys and girls were fast asleep. And many of their parents, too.

But the fourth game of this series took place under the lights, anyhow. As the rain intensified with St. Louis holding a huge lead, both teams did everything they could to turn the advantage their way. Two Cardinal baserunners got themselves deliberately thrown out on steal attempts to speed things along and get in a regulation five innings. The Tigers, on the other hand, changed pitchers, held conferences, protested the length of the sleeves on Gibson's shirt. Anything to force a delay. But no series game in history had ever been cancelled after it had begun. This was to be no exception. Despite a seventy-four-minute halt, it slopped through to its messy conclusion.

In fact, the most exciting thing that had happened had been the singing of the National Anthem before the game. Jose Feliciano had been the guest soloist. The blind Puerto Rican singer was invited to do the honors by radio announcer Ernie Harwell. Feliciano had a big hit with a blues-tinged rendition of the Doors' "Light My Fire," the same song that had been number one in the country during the week of the riots in 1967. Now Feliciano's version of the anthem reignited the flames.

Rock and soul and gospel and Native American and klezmer versions of "The Star-Spangled Banner" have since become cliches. It's impossible to predict how it will come out before any given athletic event. But in 1968 the song was regarded as untouchable. Robert Goulet had been severely criticized a few years before for simply forgetting some of the words when he sang it before a championship fight. Rocking the anthem was unthinkable. You sang it straight. Motown's Marvin Gaye had delivered it that way when it was his turn to sing.

But as Feliciano sang the opening bars, it quickly became apparent that this was not going to be the same old anthem. In fact, no one was quite sure what it was. The words were familiar. But the melody had been deconstructed into a seemingly random hodge-podge of chords and vocal gymnastics.

Feliciano received a rippling of polite applause as he left the field with his leader dog. Most of the crowd sat in silence, not quite knowing what they had just heard. But the television audience knew. It was sacrilege, a deliberate mocking of American values and our fighting men overseas. The telephone lines lit up beyond the capacity of stadium operators to handle the calls. Other outraged viewers called their local TV affiliates or the commissioner's office or a newspaper. In their minds, the protest movement had invaded the World Series and sullied the flag in full view of millions.

Feliciano was stunned and a little put out by the reaction. He explained that he had meant no disrespect. It was just his interpretation of the song. He treated it with his musical sensibilities. He even criticized Gaye for not having the courage to perform the anthem out of his own musical background. There would not be such a political flap over a pregame ceremony until a marine unit walked onto the field in Atlanta holding the Canadian flag upside down in 1992.

When Cepeda connected right away in game five, it looked like the Tigers were as scrambled as Feliciano's chords. Another drubbing was coming right up. But slowly, laboriously, Detroit crawled back into it. Freehan even managed to throw out Brock on an attempted steal. Triples by Stanley and Horton and a routine Northrup grounder that suddenly took a fluke hop over Javier's head cut the St. Louis lead to 3–2 in the fourth.

Brock then started the fifth with his third straight hit of the game, a double against the wall in left. Javier followed with a single, and it seemed that the Cards were on the wing again. Horton had been taken out of game two in the late innings because Mayo had expressed doubts about the strength of his arm. Horton hadn't liked that and felt that his abilities had been unfairly maligned. Now he charged Javier's single and attempted the impossible— throwing out Brock at the plate.

It was Freehan's call on whether to have Wert cut off the throw or let it go through. He said nothing, and Horton's bullet came to him on one hop, just as Brock arrived. But Brock was standing up. Just as the Tigers had noted in their scouting reports, Brock was so used to running unmolested that he never dreamed an attempt would be made on him. A slide would have put him in under any tag. Instead, Freehan's body bumped the running Brock off the plate. The catcher immediately whirled and tagged Brock, and plate umpire Doug Harvey emphatically called Brock out. The Cards descended on Harvey in a screaming mass, protesting that Brock's foot had reached the plate. After repeatedly viewing replays from every angle, it is clear that Harvey made the right call. But he did it in a flash, and that decision turned the World Series around.

Never had a series swung so completely on one play. Before the play on Brock, it had been virtually all St. Louis. Detroit had staggered and stumbled, almost going turtle in a defensive posture. Now the swagger returned.

Still, into the seventh the Cards clung behind Briles to the 3–2 lead. Wert struck out, and the crowd waited to see who would come up to hit for Lolich. Despite his game-two home run, Lolich was no hitter. His average for the year was .114, and that was fairly close to his career mark. There was no logical reason to let him bat with just eight outs to go until final defeat. Especially with Gates Brown on the bench. In its own way, letting Lolich bat was as unorthodox a move as the shift of Stanley.

Once more, however, Mayo had guessed right. Lolich sent a weak pop fly to right and it fell safely for a single. The Cards immediately went to their top reliever, left-hander Joe Hoerner.

He had saved seventeen games for them during the year and compiled an ERA almost as low as Gibson's. His job was to get McAuliffe, who usually had big problems with side-arming lefties. But McAuliffe managed to get a bat on the ball and sent it on the ground into right. Stanley then walked. With the bases loaded, Kaline came to bat.

In Kaline's long career, this may have been the defining moment. Many of the corporate and VIP fans who had been given tickets for the first two games of the Series had jumped off the boat for this one. The people who loved the game were in the ballpark this Monday, and they screamed for their long-time hero with a passion that could not be contained. This is where it had all been leading, their adulation of him for all these long hopeless seasons. It was all this moment. Kaline could not fail them now.

If there had been noisy afternoons before in this ballpark's long history, they were eclipsed by the din that filled it at this moment. The light towers seemed to sway from the sheer volume of it. The big crowd pleaded with him not to fail them now. Hoerner got ahead on the count, and Kaline fouled off one pitch after another on the corners. This was Six, one of the smartest hitters in baseball, fully focused on what had to be done. Hoerner finally made one pitch a little too good. Kaline, who always described himself as "a mistake hitter," pounced on this mistake. He lined it to right-center. Lolich and McAuliffe came racing home, and the Tigers were ahead.

If there had been noise before in this game, in this season, it was nothing compared to this. The stands had become a cauldron of hysteria. The Line had come through with everything on the line. The last fifteen years had been redeemed, stamped "paid in full."

Cash added another run-scoring single off a flustered Hoerner, and Lolich closed it out for a 5–3 win. The Tigers were still alive, and the games would return to St. Louis.

CHAPTER 31

Grand Finale

It turned out that Denny McLain had a slight amendment to make to his pronouncement that his season was over.

"My shoulder isn't that bad," he told sportswriter Wells Twombley after game five. "If Mayo needs me, I'll be ready to start the sixth game."

Then why, Twombley asked McLain, had he given out the bum information about his arm the day before.

"Oh, that," said Denny, according to Twombley. "I was just trying to get back at one of the Detroit writers—the little, curly-haired Jew cocksucker."

With one important exception, that described me. Dave Nightingale, baseball writer for the *Chicago Daily News*, reported that McLain had said the same thing to him, without some of the more colorful descriptive phrases.

My inclination was to let it slide. It sounded like Denny just shooting his mouth off and not meaning anything by it, especially because I hadn't been the one to whom he had given the story. It all was an ex post facto rationale for being caught telling another whopper.

But Joe Falls was infuriated. Falls, a practicing Catholic, was often mistaken for being Jewish because of his New York accent and biting, incisive wit. When the story got back to him, he insisted that we both go down to the Detroit clubhouse after the off-day practice between games five and six and confront McLain.

So in the middle of a World Series in which the Tigers had just won one of the most dramatic games in franchise history, Falls and I found ourselves standing in front of McLain's locker and accusing him of being a lying anti-Semite. This was great fun.

McLain heatedly denied that he had said any such thing and flatly refused to offer any apology. Moreover, he said, if he would try to show up anybody it would be Falls. Joe just as adamantly said that he would not tolerate this kind of talk and demanded the apology. Falls was a pretty big guy, and McLain was getting hot, and I was frightened to death that one of them would swing on the other one. If Falls went down I would be honor bound to try to deck McLain . . . and he would have killed me. Even worse, if McLain had hurt his hand swinging at one of us we would have been blamed for blowing the World Series for the Tigers.

Several of the players, most noticeably Wilson, came rushing up to separate everyone. Mayo had heard the commotion in his office, and he came running out, too. He got between McLain and the press and asked for Falls and me to accompany him into his private office. Then he shut the doors and looked at us.

"Boys," he said. "I'm going to tell you something my daddy back in Missouri told me a long time ago. Never get into a pissing match with a skunk."

With those words of wisdom ringing in our ears, we boarded the plane for the flight back to St. Louis.

As it turned out, McLain was more than ready to go out for a third time to get the best of the Cards. Only this time there was no Gibson glowering at him. And the Tigers were fully able to come to his aid.

Detroit rose up in the third inning and, against four St. Louis pitchers, tied a series record to score 10 times. Northrup capped the scoring off with yet another grand slam, his fifth of the season. The final score was 13–1, and it was, in the words of Curt Flood, "just an old-fashioned butt-kicking." The margin of victory was the biggest in the series since the Yankees whipped Pittsburgh 16–3 in 1960. But, as many hastened to point out, the Pirates won that series.

But St. Louis still had one more card to play. Gibson was ready to pitch game seven. His series-winning streak had now grown to a record seven straight. He would be working on a full three days' rest. Although he said he was a little tired and "would rather not have to pitch," he would, nonetheless, be there. Lolich was coming back on just two days of rest, and despite two gallant performances, no one thought he could match up against Gibson. Las Vegas made the Cards 8–5 favorites.

The Busch Stadium crowd rose and gave Gibson an ovation as he walked to the bull pen to start his warm-ups. Confetti had already been prepared in the city's downtown office buildings for the victory celebration that would surely follow.

This again was the Gibson the Tigers feared. In the last series game he would ever pitch, he was once more a magnificent figure, fury in red and white. Through six innings, only one Detroit player reached base. Inning after inning, Gibson mowed them down, just as he had in his first two games.

But this time Lolich stayed with him. Matching Gibson almost pitch for pitch, the lefty had given up just two harmless singles. Then the tormentor, Brock, singled to start the sixth. Everyone knew what would come next. The St. Louis fans were screaming for it, the steal that would break the record, would set up the winning run, would finally make this persistent Detroit team come apart at the seams. Brock edged farther and farther off the bag, daring Lolich to throw the ball to the plate or to make a try for him. Finally, detecting what he thought was the start of Lolich's delivery, he took off for second. Instead, Lolich threw to first. Cash rifled a perfect throw to Stanley, who was covering the bag like a veteran. Brock was tagged out.

Then Flood also singled. He had been only slightly less aggressive than Brock on the bases, stealing three times in the series. He, too, started a mind game with Lolich, trying to force the pitcher out of his rhythm, to divert him into thinking of something besides the hitter. And once more Lolich's throw went to first. Flood, too, had been picked off. Six innings were complete, and the score remained 0–0.

In two cities, millions sat in front of their television sets, barely able to speak because of the tension. No seventh game had ever gone this far without a release, without one team grabbing some kind of advantage. (None would until Minnesota's Jack Morris won the 1991 series with a ten-inning, 1–0 win over Atlanta.) Normal life slowed to a halt on this golden Thursday afternoon in Detroit, St. Louis, and much of the rest of the nation, too. The drama at Busch Stadium was all that mattered.

Gibson began the seventh by disposing of Stanley and Kaline. Cash then got Detroit's second hit, a hard single to right. Gibson, mildly annoyed, went to work on Horton. Willie drove the ball past shortstop into left field. Now there were two on and Northrup coming to bat.

What happened next has been debated endlessly for three decades. There were deep afternoon shadows, and there were white shirts in the stands behind home, both making it hard to pick up a batted ball. The turf also was soft. A pro football game had been played there on Sunday, followed by two days of rain. But when the liner to center left Northrup's bat, it appeared that Flood, one of the best defensive outfielders in the game, would get to it without much trouble. The ball was hit hard but seemingly right at him and a little behind him. Flood took one quick step in, then tried to pivot, almost dropping to one knee. By then it was too late. The ball was over his head, and Northrup was racing into third with a two-run triple.

Flood said after the game that he had misjudged the ball, that he should have caught it. But in a book written several years later he indicated that he might not have been able to catch up to it even if he had broken back immediately. This is the version Northrup prefers.

"I know in my heart that ball was past him from the get-go," Northrup says. "My daughter told me that she read Flood's book and that it would do me good to get it. But I know what happened. Hit all the way."

In Busch Stadium, a gasp of disbelief went through the capacity crowd. This wasn't how it was supposed to go at all. A bit more than five hundred miles to the northeast, Detroiters came to their feet, also incredulous at what they were seeing on their television screens. With an almost audible whoosh, the tension drained from the day. The city began to breathe again. Now it was almost a matter of counting it down.

"I was absolutely sure we were going to win that game," says Gibson. "I knew that Lolich wasn't exactly what you'd call a finely tuned athlete. He had to be dog-tired coming back on two days' rest. I was tired, too, but I'd been through this before.

"McCarver said later that maybe in the back of their minds, the guys let it affect their attitude in games five and six because they knew they had me coming out to pitch the seventh. But it's dangerous to allow a team to gain momentum in any situation. That's what we let the Tigers do.

"When Northrup hit the ball, I was confident Flood would get it. When he came back to the dugout, he apologized, saying it was his fault. But how can you blame the best centerfielder in the business? Curt Flood was the Cardinals. And Northrup hit the damn ball four hundred feet. I would never second guess."

A moment later, Freehan, with only his second hit of the series, doubled to the left-field corner for the third run of the inning. Gibson had lost it all at once. Now there were just nine outs for Lolich to get.

The Tigers added one more run in the ninth, and Lolich kept chugging away, giving up no hits. Three to go. Flood popped to shortstop. Cepeda fouled to Freehan. Then with everyone poised for the ending, Shannon finally reached Lolich for a home run. It was the first run that St. Louis had scored off Lolich in sixteen innings, and only the second that it had managed overall since Cepeda's blast in the first inning of game five. That now seemed like a very long time ago.

Then it was McCarver. He lifted a little pop fly to the right of home plate. Freehan flung aside his mask, settled under it, and tucked away Detroit's third world championship. It was 4:06 P.M. in Detroit. The real Magic Moment had struck.

CHAPTER 32

Celebration

As McCarver's pop fly settled into Freehan's big mitt, Harry Grossman, watching the game in his Detroit apartment, suddenly began to cry. His wife, Laura, who had spilled the drinks all over the room when Matchick hit his home run in July, watched with concern. "Harry," she said. "It's only a game."

"You don't understand," he replied softly. "You don't understand."

The city erupted within minutes of the final out. Secretaries and lawyers and janitors came streaming out of the downtown skyscrapers, shrieking and laughing and crying all at once. No further work would be done on this day. A man in his late twenties, hair askew and tie removed, shouted at a reporter, "All my life I've waited for this day." Someone had ordered the fire trucks from the station in the city's financial district into the streets. They sat at the curb, sounding their sirens as shredded paper began to rain from the windows on the upper floors.

Blanche Chapp watched the ball game end and searched for an

appropriate response. As a young girl, she had lost a job because someone had given her a ticket to a 1934 series game and she had gone there instead of to work. She could not let this moment pass. She suddenly remembered that years ago someone had given her a Tiger outfit as a Halloween costume. Blanche rummaged through the closet until she found it, got into the car, and sped to the office where her daughter, Carol, worked. Carol put on the suit and walked out into the streets of downtown, the living embodiment of the Tigers, accepting congratulations and occasional hugs from everyone she passed. "It was a great way to get the feel of the crowd, and vice versa," she said.

Fred Steinhardt, who had partied at the Lindell A. C. the night the team won the pennant, watched the game in a private club downtown. "The moment the game ended, the guy standing next to me, who was about my own age, put his hand on my shoulder and said, 'There will never be another sports experience in our lives that will match this.' I never forgot that. And after all these years, you know, he was right."

The city's celebration in 1935 was legendary. But the soiree of 1968 soon eclipsed even that swell party. Within half an hour, every street in downtown was clogged with pedestrians. Cars with revelers draped over their hoods inched their way forward in the mob. No one cared. They didn't want to go anywhere else. Beers were passed from car to car, as were cigarettes of the illegal variety.

In the suburbs, people who hadn't been downtown in months jumped into their cars and headed there on the freeways, pulled irresistibly to get in on the party. In the quiet suburb of Birmingham, an elderly widow, living alone, went into her garage and sounded her car horn as her own way of being part of it.

Many observers noted that the racial suspicions that had clouded life in the city finally seemed to lift in the flow of energy and joy. *Free Press* reporter Barbara Stanton, sent out to do a story on the mood of the city, found herself walking in step with an elderly black man. He smiled and looked at her. "Everybody," he said. "Everybody."

Cars loaded with young black people from the neighborhoods surrounding downtown soon joined the flow. "Tell the world, Tigers the greatest," one young man kept yelling at the top of his lungs. "Tell the world."

The players were staging their own exercise in hilarity in St. Louis. After the final pop fly, Lolich had leaped into Freehan's arms, and the catcher, toting his burden, staggered back toward the middle of the diamond. Within a few steps the two were engulfed by the rest of the Tigers, howling and shouting in the eerie quiet that engulfed Busch Stadium.

It was the third time in a seven-game World Series that a team had come back from a 3-1 deficit. The Pirates had done it in 1925 and the Yankees in 1958—against the Braves of Mathews and McMahon. Now those two men, who had tasted the bitter potion of such a comeback, swigged the champagne of triumph.

In the clubhouse, McLain stood on a platform put up for TV interviews and sprayed the bubbly at anyone within range. Horton shook his head and kept repeating, "I looked over the left-field roof in that seventh inning, and there was Rudolph the Red-Nosed Reindeer. I have never been so happy in my life."

"What a nine," Earl Wilson shouted, marching around the room with his champagne. "What a nine."

Even staid John Fetzer, the owner who never intruded, rushed into the clubhouse, grabbed a bottle from the hands of Stanley with a quick "Gimme that," and proceeded to pour it down his throat. Jim Campbell had come to the game wearing a lucky hat, a yellow fedora. McAuliffe grabbed it from the general manager's head and put it on his own, and now it, too, was soaked with champagne. "It was when Mickey picked off Brock," McAuliffe yelled over the tumult. "That was the ball game. We'd talked about it, and Mickey knew he had to make Brock make the first move. He played it perfectly."

Mayo Smith smiled and answered questions, but his hands were shaking as he tried to light a cigarette. After all those long and weary years, drifting through the minors, playing for peanuts, getting the chances and failing, washed up—after all that, it had finally come to him. He had climbed to the top of the only mountain he ever wanted to conquer. At fifty-three, it was Mayo's turn to taste the wine.

Julio Moreno, who had gone through the season as batting practice pitcher, sat by himself with a small smile on his face. During home games he would dress and leave the park as soon as his job was done. He hadn't been around for the pennant-clinching bash. Moreno hadn't varied his routine. He sat there, dressed in his suit and tie, a part of this team, and yet not really. But on this day everyone belonged. Stanley and McAuliffe sneaked up behind him, picked him up, and deposited him fully clothed into the whirlpool as Moreno howled in delight.

Horton circled the room singing "Jingle Bells." Sparma and Warden emptied champagne bottles at each other in a squirting match from a distance of twenty paces.

Stan Musial walked over from the Cards clubhouse and grabbed Mayo in a warm embrace. "You deserve it, you son of a gun," he said. Mayo started to offer him a cup of champagne and then pulled it back. "Naw, you got plenty of this in your own restaurant," he said. "Go drink it there."

The two men then threw back their heads and laughed. Musial had known this celebration three times as a player and twice as an executive. Now an old friend had joined him on the platform, and the moment was fine.

Down the hall, the Cardinals were quietly sipping their own champagne. "I never had a bad glass," said Schoendienst. "Besides, we had a terrific season, and we lost to a good baseball team." In the streets of St. Louis, office workers who had prepared to shower confetti in celebration tossed it out the windows anyhow. Cleaning trucks moved slowly through the deserted streets after dark, tidying up the mess.

Detroit had gone way past the confetti stage. As evening approached, thousands of the celebrants, as if drawn by voices that only they could hear, got onto the freeway and started driving to Metro Airport. A crowd of a few hundred had been on hand when the Tigers had returned from St. Louis the first time. This time there would be 100,000.

Neil and Mark Hertzberg were among those who made the drive. The two brothers, who are now both physicians, decided to make the trip on impulse. "It just seemed like the right thing to do at the time," says Neil. "Emotions were running so high, you had to do something. Watching them get off the plane was a great idea. I don't think anyone dreamed that the same idea would occur to everyone else in the city."

The Tigers' plane was due at the United Airlines terminal about four hours after the game ended. Long before then, their welcoming committee brought airport traffic to a complete standstill. All parking lots were full. People simply abandoned their vehicles at the side of the entrance road or the freeway and raced toward the runway. A United flight from Denver landed, and word spread through the crowd that it was the Tigers. The crowd broke down a fence and dashed toward the taxiing plane. "I looked out the window," one astonished passenger later told a reporter, "and I saw that mob surrounding the plane, and I thought to myself, 'It's finally happened. It's the revolution.'"

Air traffic controllers finally advised airport administrators that they would have to shut down. The situation was out of control. Word was radioed to the Tigers' jet, still several minutes out of Detroit, to divert to Willow Run Airport. This facility, on the site of the World War II bomber factory, had been the city's major airport for years but had been closed to commercial flights two years before. The players landed there in almost total calm and boarded buses for the drive back to the city they had levitated.

Several Detroit journalists had so much to write after the ball game that it was impossible to make an air connection back to Detroit. They wound up at Tony's Restaurant in St. Louis for dinner and a quiet celebration. Baltimore manager Earl Weaver, who had pursued the Tigers for most of the season, seemed to be as thrilled as anyone in Detroit about the series. He kept running up with radio reports about what was going on in Detroit.

"They had to close the airport," he shouted. "Isn't that fantas-tic? God, that's just great."

The Tigers peered from the bus windows as they slowly made their way through the city streets, which were still filled with a party that didn't want to end. A few players had their eyes closed and snored, overcome with champagne and emotional release. Norm Cash had passed up the homecoming in favor of a quicker return to his own home in Texas. But most of the players looked out the windows, as if trying to engrave the scene on their mem-ory for the rest of their lives.

There were a few scattered reports of violence during the night. But almost no looting or gunplay. At Wayne State University, however, a fight broke out between two groups of stu-dents at dinnertime in the Student Center. The fight, apparent-ly, had been divided along racial lines. A few days later, the stu-dent newspaper, The South End, reported on the incident.

"The fight began," it said, "when a group of black students objected to the way in which white students were celebrating the defeat of the St. Louis Cardinals, a great black team."

Had nothing, finally, been learned?

CHAPTER 33

After the Ball

A few days later, Lolich was flown into New York for lunch at Mama Leone's and the presentation of a new Dodge Charger for being World Series MVP. He, too, was headed for Las Vegas and would perform right down the Strip from McLain and his mellow organ. Lolich worked up an act with local sportscaster and singer Jim Hendricks. In a tux and shiny patent shoes Lolich would get up in the lounge of the Frontier Hotel and, to the tune of "Goin' to Kansas City," sing about going to "St. Looee" and getting himself some birdies.

McLain took the opportunity to remark to his audience at the Riviera Hotel that "I wouldn't trade twelve Mickey Loliches for one Bob Gibson." Upon reflection, McLain decided that that hadn't come out right. So he tried it another way. "What I meant to say was that I wouldn't trade one Bob Gibson for twelve Mickey Loliches." Oh, well. On the third try he got it right.

The rest of the Tigers spent the winter of their content away from the spotlight. Mathews already had announced his retirement, and it pretty much severed his connection with Detroit. He would always be identified as a member of the Braves. He briefly managed that franchise in Atlanta and was in the dugout the night his old teammate, Henry Aaron, broke Babe Ruth's career home-run record. Although Mathews remains widely admired by his former teammates with the Tigers, he has almost no contact with them and lives quietly outside of San Diego.

On the day after Lolich accepted his car, Warden and Oyler were selected by Kansas City and Seattle in the American League expansion draft. But the core of the ball club—all five outfielders, Cash, McAuliffe, Freehan, Lolich, and Hiller—would remain to win the 1972 Eastern Division race. They lost to Oakland in a bitter five-game playoff, which they still maintain was stolen from them on a close play at first base because of umpire John Rice's hatred of Billy Martin. They never won another pennant.

"Baltimore was just too good in those years," says Northrup. "They had a little too much of everything for us. The funny thing is I wound up playing with the Orioles. I went into the clubhouse the first day and said real loud, "Clubbie, you gave me the wrong uniform. I wear number five." Brooks Robinson [whose number that was] never even looked up and said: 'Not on this team, you don't.' We got along real well. I like to think I loosened him up a little. The Orioles were a great team, but I don't think they had as much fun as we did."

Baltimore finished nineteen games ahead of the second-place Tigers in the first season of divisional play in 1969. Detroit dropped all the way to fourth place in 1970, and Mayo Smith was fired right after the season ended.

"We quit like dogs," said Northrup.

"The fans in this city wouldn't know a ballplayer from a Japanese aviator," observed Mayo upon departing, a remark that remains as cryptic as it was the day he uttered it.

McLain won his second consecutive Cy Young Award with a 24–9 season in 1969. But toward the end of the year, *Detroit*

News columnist Pete Waldmier wrote about the mysterious injury that had put McLain out of the 1967 pennant race. According to Waldmier's version of events, McLain had tried to back out of some gambling debts. A top local Mafioso paid him a visit at home and, to show McLain the error of his ways, stomped him on the foot. It may have been the only time in history a team lost a pennant to the Cosa Nostra. McLain was observed by several reporters placing bets on basketball games over the clubhouse phone in Lakeland during spring training in 1969. Some of them met privately with Jim Campbell to tell him what they had seen. Nothing ever came of it.

But in February 1970, it was announced that McLain was the target of a gambling investigation. He was suspended by the commissioner's office for several months, filled the ballpark upon his return that summer, was plagued by a chronic sore shoulder, struggled on the mound, and finally ended his performance by dumping pails of water over the heads of the city's two baseball writers, Jim Hawkins and Watson Spoelstra. The Tigers suspended McLain for the rest of the year. During the off-season, he was traded to Washington in a brilliant maneuver that gave the Tigers two starting infielders—Eddie Brinkman and Aurelio Rodriguez—and a top pitcher in Joe Coleman. The trade put Detroit in position to win the division two years later.

The team contended again in 1973 before falling out of the race in September. The end came the following year. McAuliffe was traded to Boston, Northrup was waived to Montreal, and Cash was released. In 1975 they finished last with the worst record in baseball.

Only one member of the team ever returned to the series as a player. Pat Dobson was traded after the 1969 season and found his way to Baltimore two years later. He was a twenty-game winner with the Orioles in 1971 and started against Pittsburgh in the series.

Horton also enjoyed a brief success after leaving Detroit. He wound up with Seattle in 1979 and had one of the best years of his career, with 106 RBIs. He was known there as "the Ancient Mariner" and made his home in the Northwest for a few years before returning to Detroit.

Most members of that team, however, spent their best years with the Tigers. Many of them did well financially after leaving the game, making comfortable livings in business or broadcasting. A few became quite wealthy. But some could never quite put behind the baseball life, and others paid a high price for it.

Oyler died of a heart attack at the age of forty-two. He had moved to the Seattle area after being drafted by that team and worked for Boeing after his retirement. As in Detroit, he became a semilegendary figure because of his inability to hit. He retired during the 1970 season with a lifetime average of .175. "He never carried a grudge about my replacing him during the series," said Stanley. "He was simply a great guy."

Sparma died of a heart attack at the age of forty-four. He was struck by a massive coronary in a Columbus hospital just days after undergoing a triple bypass. He never regained the touch that he displayed the night the Tigers clinched the pennant. He won just seven more games in his career and was out of baseball at the age of twenty-eight. One of the last phone calls he received in the hospital was from Earl Wilson, the man he had been called in to replace in the pennant-clinching game. Sparma's sister told reporters that the call had cheered him up immensely.

Hiller had his heart attack at the age of twenty-seven but recovered and fought his way back to the majors. McMahon, who went on to become an assistant to his childhood buddy, Al Davis, owner of the NFL's Raiders, died of a heart attack at the age of fifty-seven.

But for most of the Tigers, an entire era seemed to end when their center of laughter, Norm Cash, fell off the end of a dock and drowned in Lake Michigan. He had taken a boat to Beaver Island with his wife. After a social evening in one of the island's inns, he told his companions that he was heading back for his boat. Friends noted that it had been raining, the dock was slippery, and he was wearing cowboy boots. His body was found in fifteen feet of water near the dock the next morning. It was eighteen years and two days after the final game of the 1968 World Series.

Although he had been a target of boos throughout his playing days, Cash was treated with deep affection and regard after his retirement. He moved to Detroit and came to symbolize the ethos of the '68 team: fun-loving and scrappy, indomitable, and very human. He worked as a color commentator on cable television for a few seasons. His wit and the tales he told about his illustrious teammates carried well over the tube. But he had to give it up after a stroke left his face partially paralyzed and caused him to slur his words. In an old-timer's game several months before his death, fans gasped when an easy throw from across the infield hit him in the head and bounced away. "Well, I field about as good as I always did," he said later. But he was deeply embarrassed over the incident and despondent over how the stroke had robbed him of his physical gifts. He was fifty-one at the time of his death.

McLain claimed that the Tigers had shortened his career and ruined his arm by forcing him to take cortisone shots for a chronically sore shoulder. He lost twenty-two games with Washington in 1971 and, after several attempts at a comeback with various teams, left the majors for good after 1972. He moved to Tennessee and then Florida. Both he and his wife declared bankruptcy on separate occasions to wipe out accumulated debts. In 1985, he was convicted of drug-related charges and racketeering. Sent to a federal prison, he served twenty-nine months and was released after an appeal, alleging irregularities in his trial, was upheld.

Ballooned to over 300 pounds, he returned to Detroit in the late 1980s and seemed to rebuild his life. He became the host of an early-morning radio talk show, displaying a surprising ability to gab engagingly about a wide range of subjects. His populist approach to most issues appealed to the local audience, and his ratings put him among the leaders in the highly competitive time slot. But the death of his daughter in an auto accident left him badly shaken. A dispute with his station over a new contract and his demands to broadcast from a home studio abruptly ended his media career. He then announced that he had become part-owner of a meat-packing company in the small town of Chesaning. But after a few months, the company went out of business. McLain and his partners were found guilty in December 1996 of conspiracy, fraud, and theft for raiding the company pension fund and using the money for, among other things, a down payment on a Puerto Rican condominium and an airplane for McLain. As of this writing, the case is pending trial.

You will find scant sympathy among his former teammates for the mess McLain made of his life after baseball. Most of them remain closely knit, helping each other in business when they can, keeping the friendships that were forged all those years ago. But McLain remains always the outsider. He was tolerated for the enormous talent and competitive fire he brought to the game, but regarded with suspicion, and even hostility, for his endless self-promotion. That hasn't changed.

The game itself changed enormously after 1968. It was, in many regards, the last year of its kind, a season out of time. The players staged their first walkout at the start of spring training in 1969 over pension benefits. The walkout lasted only a few days and affected very little, but it was a show of resolve. Within three years, the players walked again, and this time it took a week off of the start of the 1972 season. The game shut down for more than a month in 1981, and in 1994 the season was cancelled after mid-August, and no World Series was played. The sport is still trying to recover from the public relations disaster of that stoppage.

Curt Flood, the man who couldn't quite get to Northrup's drive in 1968, was traded by St. Louis the following season. Instead of reporting to Philadelphia, he decided to legally challenge baseball's reserve clause in the standard player contract. He was unsuccessful, and his career was sacrificed as a result. "You don't really think they would ever let a black man bring down the system," says Earl Wilson bitterly. But it was the first step in ending the old order that had kept player salaries artificially depressed. By the end of the '70s, the pendulum had swung fully to the other extreme. Million-dollar contracts were commonplace. By the '80s, individual players were making more money than the entire payroll of the American League in the 1960s. Ballplayers were paid like movie stars, and they began to act that way, too.

Drug use derailed several promising careers. The designated hitter brought specialization to a game that had always depended on multitalented generalists. The philosophy of pitching changed. The phrase "complete game" almost vanished from the game's lexicon. Now there were long relievers and short relievers and stoppers. Managers shuttled them in and out in the late innings, and the game slowed to a crawl. The three-hour ball game was almost the norm. All of it turned the game into something far different than it was in 1968. Maybe not worse. But undeniably different.

It is now extremely rare, for example, to play a World Series game in much less than three hours. But the seventh game in '68, on which everything was riding, played amid almost stifling tension, took a grand total of two hours and seven minutes.

Mayo Smith died of a stroke in 1977. He never managed again, and over the years his reputation has remained fairly unchanged. He is still regarded as a very lucky man who ended up in the right place at the right time. When a group of expatriate Tigers fans located in the Washington, D.C., area rummaged about for a suitable name for their organization—unpretentious and a bit obscure—they settled on the Mayo Smith Society. So in the nation's capital, at least, Mayo enjoys a certain kind of immortality.

In Detroit, members of the '68 Tigers remain as popular as ever. Jerry Lewis, who had thrilled to their exploits then as a young man, began holding fantasy camps featuring members of that team in the early '80s. The camps have sold out every year since. Several of his customers return annually and have become close friends with the players they once idolized. Willie Horton fires up his barbecue, old stories are told again, drinks are passed around. It's the next best thing to having been there.

Because this team still occupies a special place in the history of the city. The players have joined their predecessors of 1935 as an almost mythic unit—more than a baseball team. The belief has passed into Detroit folklore. Many people swear, as Willie Horton says, that they were "put here by God to save the city."

At the risk of sounding sacrilegious, it should be pointed out that the Almighty didn't have much of a follow-through. The city's racial split was too wide for the temporary euphoria of a championship to overcome. White flight continued unabated. The homicide rate soared, and throughout the '70s and '80s, Detroit became known as the Murder Capital of America. Landmark hotels, restaurants, theaters, stores shut down. By the mid-'80s, almost no commercial presence remained downtown. Although the suburbs prosper, Detroit's average income is the lowest of any large American city. In many respects, the '67 riots never ended.

Even with contending teams, home baseball attendance began to drop in the late 1980s. As fans moved farther and farther away, into newer and ever more distant suburbs, they became reluctant to make the long drive back to see a ball game. It soon became apparent that in order to survive and generate the revenue needed to compete in the world of free agency, Tiger Stadium would have to be replaced. In spite of the history associated with the site, the only one on which the Tigers had ever played, plans were approved for a new stadium. Necessity simply outweighed sentiment. The new ballpark will be closer to downtown and ready before the end of the century. There are hopes that the new ballpark will be the catalyst for a lasting redevelopment of downtown, a true rebirth of the city center.

Dick Tracewski stayed around as a coach through the end of the 1995 season, the last of the '68 Tigers to remain in uniform. Kaline and Price are still heard as television broadcasters.

Campbell, who had devoted his life to the organization, was

fired as president of the Tigers in 1992. It was a condition of the sale of the club to pizza magnate Mike Ilitch. Campbell retired to Lakeland, the training base at which he had spent so many springs. But he refused to come out to Tigertown, and he never saw the Tigers play again.

Those who knew him best said that much of his zest for living left him after his dismissal. He died in December 1995. Gates Brown was a pallbearer at the funeral, and Kaline delivered one of the eulogies. The subject was loyalty. It was a term that had become almost oxymoronic in baseball.

The bells of Mariners' Church in downtown Detroit played "Take Me Out to the Ballgame" as the casket was carried to the waiting hearse. It was just the sort of tune Campbell loved to hear at his ballpark. None of your rock and roll or that Jose Feliciano guy.

But as the old bells tolled, it sounded like a dirge for a vanished game. Hunched against the December cold, the mourners walked off into the wintry, empty streets of Detroit.

Statistics

THE 1968 TIGERS—GAME BY GAME

4/10	L	Boston	3–7	L-Wilson	W-Ellsworth	0–1	T6	1
4/11	W	Boston	4–3	W-Warden	L-Wyatt	1–1	T4	1
4/13	W	Chicago	5–2	W-Patterson	L-Peters	2–1	T3	1
4/14	W	Chicago	5–4	W-Lasher	L-Locker	3–1	2	1
4/16	W	@Boston	9–2	W-Wilson	L-Culp	4–1	2	1
4/17	W	Cleve.	4–3	W-Warden	L-Fisher	5–1	2	1
4/18	W	Cleve.	5–0	W-Sparma	L-Hargan	6–1	T1	2
4/20	W	@Chicago	4–1	W-Warden	L-Wood	7–1	1	1
4/21	W	@Chicago	4–1	W-Wilson	L-Horlen	8–1		
	W	@Chicago	4–2	W-McLain	L-Carlos	9–1	1	1½
4/24	L	@Cleve.	0–2	L-Sparma	W-Hargan	9–2	1	2
4/26	L	@New York	0–5	L-Wilson	L-Stottlemyre	9–3	1	1½
4/27	W	@New York	7–0	W-McLain	L-Peterson	10–3	1	1½
4/28	L	@New York	1–2	L-Sparma	W-Monbouquette	10–4		
	W	@New York	3–2	W-Hiller	L-Womack	11–4	1	2
4/29	W	Oakland	2–1	W-Lolich	L-Aker	12–4	1	2
4/30	L	Oakland	1–3	L-Wilson	W-Lindblad	12–5	1	½
5/1	W	Minnesota	3–2	W-McLain	L-Merritt	13–5	1	1½
5/2	L	Minnesota	2–3	L-Ribant	W-Chance	13–6	1	½
5/3	L	Calif.	5–6	L-Lolich	W-Hamilton	13–7	2	½
5/4	L	Calif.	2–7	L-Wilson	W-McGlothlin	13–8	2	1½
5/5	W	Calif.	5–2	W-McLain	L-Brunet	14–8	2	1½
5/6	L	@Balt.	0–4	L-Sparma	W-Leonhard	14–9	2	2½
5/7	W	@Balt.	2–1	W-Lolich	L-Phoebus	15–9	2	1½
5/8	W	@Balt.	3–1	W-Wilson	L-McNally	16–9	2	½
5/10	W	@Wash.	12–1	W-McLain	L-Moore	17–9	1	½
5/11	W	@Wash.	12–2	W-Sparma	L-Bertaina	18–9	1	1½
5/12	L	@Wash.	3–6	L-Patterson	W-Coleman	18–10	1	2
5/14	W	Balt.	4–0	W-Wilson	L-McNally	19–10	1	2
5/15	L	Balt.	8–10	L-McLain	W-Watt	19–11	1	1½
5/17	W	Wash.	7–3	W-Sparma	L-Jones	20–11	1	2
5/18	L	Wash.	4–8	L-Lolich	W-Bertaina	20–12	1	2
5/19	W	Wash.	5–4	W-Lasher	L-Jones	21–12		
	W	Wash.	7–0	W-Cain	L-Pascual	22–12	1	2
5/20	W	@Minn.	4–3	W-McLain	L-Merritt	23–12	1	2½

5/21	L	@Minn.	1–3	L-Sparma	W-Chance	23–13	1	2
5/22	L	@Minn.	3–4	L-Lasher	W-Perranoski	23–14	1	2
5/24	T	@Oakland	2–2				1	2
5/25	W	@Oakland	2–1	W-McLain	L-Krausse	24–14	1	2
5/26	L	@Oakland	6–7	L-Hiller	W-Lindblad	24–15	1	1
5/27	L	@Calif.	6–7	L-Patterson	W-Wright	24–16	1	½
5/28	W	@Calif.	4–1	W-Hiller	L-Brunet	25–16	1	½
5/29	W	@Calif.	3–0	W-McLain	L-McGlothlin	26–16	1	1½
5/30	W	@Calif.	7–3	W-Sparma	L-Clark	27–16	1	1½
5/31	W	New York	1–0	W-Lolich	L-Stottlemyre	28–16	1	2½
6/1	W	New York	5–4	W-Lasher	L-Womack	29–16	1	2½
6/2	L	New York	3–4	L-Warden	W-Verbanic	29–17		
	W	New York	8–1	W-Hiller	L-Barber	30–17	1	3
6/3	L	@Boston	3–4	L-Sparma	W-Santiago	30–18	1	2
6/4	L	@Boston	0–2	L-Lolich	W-Bell	30–19		
	W	@Boston	2–0	W-Dobson	L-Waslewski	31–19	1	2½
6/5	W	@Boston	5–4	W-McLain	L-Landis	32–19	1	2½
6/6	W	@Boston	5–3	W-Sparma	L-Stange	33–19	1	2½
6/7	W	Cleve.	5–4	W-Lasher	L-Paul	34–19	1	3½
6/8	W	Cleve.	3–1	W-Lolich	L-McDowell	35–19	1	4½
6/9	L	Cleve.	0–2	L-McLain	W-Tiant	35–20	1	3½
6/11	W	Minn.	3–1	W-Dobson	L-Chance	36–20		
	W	Minn.	3–2	W-Hiller	L-Worthington	37–20	1	4½
6/12	W	Minn	2–1	W-Lolich	L-Kaat	38–20	1	5
6/13	W	Minn.	3–1	W-McLain	L-Merritt	39–20	1	5½
6/14	W	@Chicago	6–5	W-Hiller	L-Priddy	40–20	1	6½
6/15	L	@Chicago	4–7	L-Sparma	W-John	40–21	1	6½
6/16	L	@Chicago	2–3	L-Lolich	W-Wilhelm	40–22		
	W	@Chicago	6–1	W-McLain	L-Carlos	41–22	1	7½
6/18	W	Boston	2–1	W-Wilson	L-Santiago	42–22	1	8
6/19	L	Boston	5–8	L-Sparma	W-Landis	42–23	1	7½
6/20	W	Boston	5–1	W-McLain	L-Ellsworth	43–23	1	8½
6/21	L	@Cleve.	3–4	L-Dobson	W-Fisher	43–24	1	7½
6/22	L	@Cleve.	0–2	L-Wilson	W-Hargan	43–25	1	6½
6/23	L	@Cleve.	0–3	L-Hiller	W-Tiant	43–26		
	W	@Cleve.	4–1	W-Sparma	L-McDowell	44–26	1	6½
6/24	W	@Cleve.	14–3	W-McLain	L-Paul	45–26	1	7½
6/25	W	@New York	8–5	W-Ribant	L-Monbouquette	46–26	1	7½
6/28	W	Chicago	5–4	W-Lasher	L-Wood	47–26	1	8
6/29	W	Chicago	5–2	W-McLain	L-Carlos	48–26	1	8½
6/30	L	Chicago	0–12	L-Sparma	W-John	48–27	1	7½

7/1	W	Calif.	5–1	W-Lolich	L-Brunet	49–27	1	7½
7/2	W	Calif.	3–1	W-Wilson	L-Murphy	50–27	1	8½
7/3	W	Calif.	5–2	W-McLain	L-McGlothlin	51–27	1	8½
7/4	W	Calif.	13–10	W-Ribant	L-Burgmeier	52–27	1	8½
7/5	W	Oakland	8–5	W-Lolich	L-Hunter	53–27	1	8½
7/6	L	Oakland	1–4	L-Wilson	W-Dobson	53–28	1	8½
7/7	W	Oakland	5–4	W-McLain	L-Sprague	54–28		
	W	Oakland	7–6	W-Sparma	L-Nash	55–28	1	9½

All-Star Game

7/11	L	@Minn.	4–5	L-Hiller	W-Perranoski	55–29	1	9½
7/12	W	@Minn	5–1	W-McLain	L-Kaat	56–29	1	9½
7/13	L	@Minn.	6–7	L-Ribant	W-Roland	56–30	1	8½
7/14	L	@Calif.	3–7	L-Wilson	W-Ellis	56–31	1	7½
7/15	L	@Calif.	0–4	L-Lolich	W-Brunet	56–32	1	6½
7/16	W	@Oakland	4–0	W-McLain	L-Dobson	57–32	1	6½
7/17	L	@Oakland	2–3	L-Sparma	W-Hunter	57–33	1	6½
7/18	W	@Oakland	3–1	W-Wilson	L-Krausse	58–33	1	7
7/19	W	Balt.	5–4	W-Dobson	L-Drawbowsky	59–33	1	7½
7/20	L	Balt.	3–5	L-McLain	W-McNally	59–34	1	6½
7/21	L	Balt	2–5	L-Wilson	W-Hardin	59–35		
	L	Balt.	1–4	L-Dobson	W-Phoebus	59–36	1	5½
7/23	W	@Wash.	6–4	W-McLain	L-Ortega	60–36	1	6
7/24	L	@Wash.	3–6	L-Lolich	W-Hannan	60–37	1	5
7/25	W	@Wash.	4–1	W-Sparma	L-Howard	61–37	1	5½
7/26	W	@Balt.	4–1	W-Wilson	L-Hardin	62–37	1	6½
7/27	W	@Balt.	9–0	W-McLain	L-Phoebus	63–37	1	7½
7/28	L	@Balt.	1–5	L-Lolich	W-McNally	63–38	1	6½
7/29	L	New York	2–7	L-Sparma	W-Verbanic	63–39	1	7
7/30	W	New York	5–0	W-Wilson	L-Stottlemyre	64–39	1	7
7/31	W	Wash.	4–0	W-McLain	L-Bertaina	65–39	1	7
8/1	L	Wash.	3–9	L-Dobson	W-Coleman	65–40	1	6
8/2	W	@Minn.	6–5	W-McMahon	L-Miller	66–40	1	6
8/3	L	@Minn.	0–4	L-Wilson	W-Chance	66–41	1	6
8/4	W	@Minn.	2–1	W-McLain	L-Kaat	67–41	1	6
8/6	W	Cleve.	2–1	W-Wyatt	L-Paul	68–41	1	6½
8/7	W	Cleve.	5–2	W-Lolich	L-Williams	69–41	1	6½
8/8	W	Cleve.	6–1	W-Wilson	L-McDowell	70–41	1	6½
	W	Cleve.	13–1	W-McLain	L-Siebert	71–41	1	6½
8/9	L	Boston	3–5	L-Dobson	W-Stange	71–42	1	5½

8/10	W	Boston	4–3	W-Lolich	L-Landis	72–42	1	5½
8/11	W	Boston	5–4	W-Lolich	L-Stange	73–42		
	W	Boston	6–5	W-Warden	L-Stephenson	74–42	1	7
8/12	W	@Cleve.	6–3	W-McLain	L-Romo	75–42	1	7
8/13	L	@Cleve.	0–1	L-Dobson	W-Siebert	75–43	1	6
8/14	W	@Cleve.	3–0	W-Lolich	L-Tiant	76–43	1	7
8/16	W	@Boston	4–0	W-McLain	L-Lonborg	77–43	1	8
8/17	W	@Boston	10–9	W-McMahon	L-Stange	78–43	1	8
8/18	L	@Boston	1–4	L-Wilson	W-Pizarro	78–44	1	8
8/20	W	Chicago	7–0	W-Hiller	L-Fisher	79–44		
	L	Chicago	2–10	L-McLain	W-Peters	79–45	1	7
8/21	W	Chicago	3–2	W-Patterson	L-Wood	80–45	1	7½
8/22	W	Chicago	4–2	W-Lolich	L-Ribant	81–45	1	7½
8/23	L	@New York	1–2	L-Wilson	W-Bahnsen	81–46		
	T	@New York	3–3				1	7½
8/24	L	@New York	1–2	L-McLain	W-Stottlemyre	81–47	1	6½
8/25	L	@New York	5–6	L-Patterson	W-Colavito	81–48		
	L	@New York	4–5	L-Lolich	W-Hamilton	81–49	1	5
8/26	W	@Chi. (Mil.)	3–0	W-Wilson	L-Carlos	82–49	1	5½
8/27	L	@Chicago	1–2	L-Hiller	W-Wood	82–50	1	4
8/28	W	Calif.	6–1	W-McLain	L-Burgmeier	83–50	1	5
8/29	W	Calif.	2–0	W-Lolich	L-Brunet	84–50	1	6
8/30	W	Balt.	9–1	W-Wilson	L-Phoebus	85–50	1	7
8/31	L	Balt.	1–5	L-Hiller	W-McNally	85–51	1	6
9/1	W	Balt.	7–3	W-McLain	L-Hardin	86–51	1	7
9/2	L	@Oakland	0–4	L-Lolich	W-Nash	86–52		
	W	@Oakland	4–3	W-Dobson	L-Segui	87–52	1	7
9/3	W	@Oakland	6–3	W-Dobson	L-Sprague	88–52	1	8
9/4	W	@Oakland	4–2	W-Hiller	L-Dobson	89–52	1	8
9/6	W	Minn.	8–3	W-McLain	L-Kaat	90–52	1	9
9/7	L	Minn.	1–2	L-Dobson	W-Worthington	90–53	1	8
9/8	L	Minn.	1–3	L-Wilson	W-Chance	90–54	1	7
9/9	W	@Calif.	6–0	W-Lolich	L-Bennett	91–54	1	8
9/10	W	@Calif.	7–2	W-McLain	L-Messersmith	92–54	1	8½
9/11	W	@Calif.	8–2	W-Hiller	L-Brunet	93–54	1	8
9/13	W	Oakland	3–0	W-Wilson	L-Hunter	94–54	1	9½
9/14	W	Oakland	5–4	W-McLain	L-Segui	95–54	1	9½
9/15	W	Oakland	13–0	W-Lolich	L-Krausse	96–54	1	10½
9/16	W	New York	9–1	W-Hiller	L-Verbanic	97–54	1	10½
9/17	W	New York	2–1	W-Sparma	L-Hamilton	98–54	1	11½
9/19	W	New York	6–2	W-McLain	L-Stottlemyre	99–54	1	12½

9/20	W	@Wash.	6–3	W-Lolich	L-Humphreys	100–54	1	13½
9/21	W	@Wash.	4–3	W-Sparma	L-Cox	101–54	1	13½
9/22	L	@Wash.	0–6	L-Hiller	W-Pascual	101–55	1	12½
9/23	L	@Balt.	1–2	L-McLain	W-Nelson	101–56	1	11½
9/24	W	@Balt.	5–3	W-Lolich	L-Hardin	102–56	1	12½
9/25	W	@Balt.	4–3	W-McMahon	L-Phoebus	103–56	1	13
9/27	L	Wash.	1–3	L-Dobson	W-Coleman	103–57	1	13
9/28	L	Wash.	1–2	L-McMahon	W-Humphreys	103–58	1	12½
9/29	L	Wash.	2–3	L-Dobson	W-Moore	103–59	1	12
10/2	L	@St. Louis	0–4	L-McLain	W-Gibson			
10/3	W	@St. Louis	8–1	W-Lolich	L-Briles			
10/5	L	St. Louis	3–7	L-Wilson	W-Washburn			
10/6	L	St. Louis	1–10	L-McLain	W-Gibson			
10/7	W	St. Louis	5–3	W-Lolich	L-Hoerner			
10/9	W	@St. Louis	13–1	W-McLain	L-Washburn			
10/10	W	@St. Louis	4–1	W-Lolich	L-Gibson			

THE 1968 TIGERS—THE STATS

	G	AB	R	H	2B	3B	HR	RBI	SB	Ave.	BB	SO
Brown	67	92	15	34	7	2	6	15	0	.370	12	4
Christian	3	3	0	1	1	0	0	0	0	.333	0	0
Kaline	102	327	49	94	14	1	10	53	6	.287	55	39
Horton	143	512	68	146	20	2	36	85	0	.285	49	110
Northrup	154	580	76	153	29	7	21	90	4	.264	50	87
Freehan	155	540	73	142	24	2	25	84	0	.263	65	64
Cash	127	411	50	108	15	1	25	63	1	.263	39	70
Stanley	153	583	88	151	16	6	11	60	4	.259	42	57
Green	6	4	0	1	0	0	0	0	0	.250	1	0
McAuliffe	151	570	95	142	24	10	16	56	8	.249	82	99
Mathews	31	52	4	11	0	0	3	8	0	.212	5	12
Matchick	80	227	18	46	6	2	3	14	0	.203	10	46
Wert	150	536	44	107	15	1	12	37	0	.200	37	79
Price	64	132	12	23	4	0	3	13	0	.174	13	14
Tracewski	90	212	30	33	3	1	4	15	3	.156	24	51
Oyler	111	215	13	29	6	1	1	12	0	.135	20	59
Comer	48	48	8	6	0	1	1	3	0	.125	2	7
Campbell	9	8	1	1	0	0	1	2	0	.125	1	3
Wilson	40	88	9	20	0	1	7	17	0	.227	2	35
Ribant	16	5	1	1	0	0	0	0	0	.200	1	1
McLain	44	111	7	18	1	1	0	4	0	.162	1	37

	G	AB	R	H	2B	3B	HR	RBI	SB	Ave.	BB	SO
Dobson	47	28	2	4	0	0	0	1	0	.143	2	7
Cain	8	7	0	1	1	0	0	0	0	.143	0	2
McMahon	45	7	0	1	0	0	0	0	0	.143	0	3
Sparma	34	60	2	8	1	0	0	2	0	.133	1	24
Lolich	41	70	5	8	3	0	0	3	0	.114	6	25
Lasher	34	9	0	1	0	0	0	0	0	.111	0	4
Hiller	39	37	1	3	0	0	0	2	0	.081	0	14
Face	2											
Warden	28	2	0	0	0	0	0	0	0	.000	0	1
Rooker	2	2	0	0	0	0	0	0	0	.000	0	1
Wyatt	37	3	0	0	0	0	0	0	0	.000	0	3
Patterson	38	13	0	0	0	0	0	1	0	.000	1	8

	G	GS	CG	W-L	IP	H	R	ER	BB	SO	SV	ERA
McLain	41	41	28	31–6	336	241	86	73	63	280	0	1.96
Lolich	39	32	8	17–9	220	178	84	78	65	197	1	3.19
Wilson	34	33	10	13–12	224.1	192	77	71	65	168	0	2.85
Sparma	34	31	7	10–10	182.1	169	81	75	77	110	0	3.70
Hiller	39	12	4	9–6	128	92	37	34	51	78	2	2.39
Lasher	34	0	0	5–1	48.2	37	19	18	22	32	5	3.33
Dobson	47	10	2	5–8	125	89	39	37	48	93	7	2.66
Warden	28	0	0	4–1	37.1	30	15	15	15	25	3	3.65
McMahon	20	0	0	3–1	35.2	22	8	8	10	33	1	2.02
Ribant	14	0	0	2–2	24.1	20	7	6	10	7	1	2.22
Patterson	38	1	0	2–3	68	53	19	16	27	49	7	2.12
Wyatt	22	0	0	1–0	30.1	26	9	8	11	25	1	2.37
Cain	8	4	0	1–0	24	25	9	8	20	13	0	3.00
Rooker	2	0	0	0–0	4.2	4	2	2	1	4	0	3.60
Face	2	0	0	0–0	1	2	0	0	1	1	0	0.00

Index